CH June 2016

GREAT HORSE STORIES

STORIES

Girls

REBECCA E. ONDOV

HARVEST HOUSE PUBLISHERS
EUGENE, OREGON

GREAT HORSE STORIES FOR GIRLS

Copyright © 2015 Blazing Ink, Inc.
Published by Harvest House Publishers
Eugene, Oregon 97402
www.harvesthousepublishers.com

Library of Congress Cataloging-in-Publication Data
    Ondov, Rebecca E.
    Great horse stories for girls / Rebecca E. Ondov.
        pages cm
    ISBN 978-0-7369-6237-7 (pbk.)
    ISBN 978-0-7369-6238-4 (eBook)
    1. Horsemen and horsewomen—United States—Religious life—Anecdotes. 2. Horses—United States—Anecdotes. 3. Girls—United States—Life skills guides. 4. Human–animal relationships—Religious aspects—Anecdotes. I. Title.
    BV4596.A54O524 2015
    242'.62—dc23

                                                                    2014042878

To Cindy Peterson.
Thank you for showing me how to live my faith.
Your friendship is priceless.

Acknowledgments

To God: I am forever grateful for Your grace and mercy.

To my prayer team: Thank you for all the hours you prayed for me and encouraged me.

To Harvest House Publishers: I'm thrilled to be part of your team.

To Barbara Gordon: Your wisdom adds zing to my writing. Thank you! (By the way, I can't wait till we get to the coast and hang out together. Will anyone be safe on the beach if we rent dune buggies?)

To Tom Fox, my daytime boss: Thanks for your encouragement. I appreciate you.

To Janet Kobobel Grant, my literary agent: You're a shining star! Thank you for all you do to stay on the cutting-edge of publishing.

To all my horses, mules, dogs, and cats: You've been my faithful friends.

Contents

Meet the Stars

Czar. It was love at first sight when I saw the lanky, month-old, bay colt. He grew up to become my all-time dream horse. He and I traveled thousands of miles when I took people on pack trips in the Bob Marshall Wilderness of Montana.

Czar and Rebecca*

Dancer. I bought this beautiful, sorrel, Tennessee walker mare without asking God first. What a mess I created. I'll explain later how things went really bad quickly. But, thankfully, when I asked God to fix it, He turned the situation around and blessed my socks off with Dancer.

Dancer

Dazzle. One day when I was shopping for knobs for my kitchen cupboards, I took a break and opened a classified ads paper. On the page before me was a beautiful, black Tennessee walker mare. I knew she was mine. Instead of buying knobs, I went home with a horse!

Dazzle*

Little Girl*

Little Girl. When she was two days old, Little Girl was kicked in the head by a horse and her jaw was shattered. Some ranch hands found her lying motionless in the field. They brought her to the house, and I scooped her into the car. While rushing her to the clinic, I had to stop and give her CPR three times. The vet pinned her jaw and doctored her wounds. That night I bedded her down in my kitchen. The following day I moved her into a safe shed. Over the next couple months, I milked her mom every two hours around the clock and bottle-fed Little Girl. She recovered and turned into the biggest, long-eared, love bug blessing I've ever met.

A Note
from Rebecca

Horses. Why do they take my breath away? Why does my heart pound when I catch a glimpse of them? I think it's because God tucked a special gift inside every girl's heart—the love of horses. Through horses God has taken me on an incredible journey filled with adventures I want to share with you. As we step into green pastures, I hope your love for horses will deepen. I also pray that you'll discover what a miracle you are and how much God loves you.

Blessings,

Rebecca

P.S. Would you and your friends like to use this book for a Bible study? Find out more by going to http://www.rebeccaondov.com and click on the "For Horse Girls Only" link.

1

Chosen

God said,
"Let us make human beings in our image."

Genesis 1:26 NLT

All was still in the indoor arena except for the cooing of the pigeons from the rafters and the sound of the horse's hooves digging into the sand. I sat tall in the saddle, paying attention to the sorrel-colored mare with the reddish-gold mane. Through the thick leather of the western saddle, I could feel the muscles ripple in her back. She quickly paced around the arena. Her hooves kicked up a light haze of dust that hung in the warm, spring air. My heart thumped in my chest. *Could this be the one?*

I was "trying out" a Tennessee walker (the formal name is "Tennessee Walking Horse"). I wanted to buy another riding horse. At home in my pasture stood my very old and retired saddle horse, a mule I used to pack, and a horse with joint problems that couldn't be ridden. I didn't have a saddle horse I could ride every day. In another month the snow would melt off the sides of the mountains, and horseback-riding season would start in Montana. I didn't want to miss a single day in the saddle.

I gathered the reins with my sweaty hands and gently laid them against the side of the mare's neck. Instantly she turned. Over the next hour she willingly changed gaits, stopped, and backed up. I rode her down the dirt road, and my body barely rocked side-to-side because her gait was so smooth. It was as if she was dancing on air. When I was done with the test ride, I reined her into the barn and stopped next to her wooden box stall. I stroked her neck. A grin brightened my face as I announced, "Well, girl, you passed the test. I'm choosing you!"

Dancer, Tessa, and Rebecca chitchatting.

• Just Between You and Me •

Have you thought about how exciting it is to be chosen? How do you feel when you're picked to be part of a school team? A school play? A member of the band or orchestra? Have you or one of your friends been invited to be part of a special class of some kind?

Have you noticed that the great feeling gradually fades away? Especially when the spotlight of acceptance shifts and shines on someone else?

What if instead of looking to others for approval and good feelings, you could *know* deep inside your heart that *you are important and valuable*? What if the very One who created the universe and hung the stars in place—the most powerful and important Being who ever existed—chose to create you?

The best part is that this is all true! You are a one-of-a-kind person created by God Himself. *Wow!*

Lord, help us understand how special we are to You. Amen.

• Just for Fun •

Did you know there are lots of breeds of horses? Why not make a list and see how many you can name? When you're done, look up horse breeds on the Internet. Just go to a search engine (like Google or Yahoo) and type "compare horse breeds."

If you were to choose a horse, what breed would you want and why?

2

What's in a Name?

A good name is more desirable than great riches.

Proverbs 22:1

The sorrel mare turned her head and watched me. I loosened the cinch of the western saddle sitting on her back. Her deep-brown eyes followed my every move as I slipped the saddle and blanket off. I was excited because I'd just decided to purchase her. After lugging the saddle and blanket over to the rack and hanging them in place, I walked back to her.

What am I going to name you, girl? Coming up with the right names for my animals is important to me. I want the names to reflect not just who the animal is, but what I'd like the critter to become. I enjoy thinking about names—sometimes for days or even weeks before just the right one comes to me.

Standing next to the mare, I stroked her soft, red coat. She sighed, lowered her head, and dozed. I considered what I would call her. My mind reviewed the ride I'd just taken. I'd never been on a horse whose gaits were so smooth. I felt she'd been dancing on air. I inhaled excitedly. "That's it! Your name needs to be Dancer!" The mare woke up, curled her head around, and batted her red eyelashes at me. I was sure she was agreeing with me.

· Just Between You and Me ·

Names are more than just the sounds of letters strung together. We attach meanings to them. We often view them as clues that tell us what's inside the person. When I hear some people's names I think, *She's probably considerate* or *He's probably helpful*. Have you ever heard someone's name and shuddered because words like "bossy" or "rude" immediately came to mind? That's the wonderful and horrible thing about names.

Unlike a horse, who doesn't have a choice in what they become, we humans make our own decisions. We've been given a wonderful gift from God—the ability to decide how we'll act and who we'll become. Through those decisions, we're choosing what our names will mean to those around us.

When someone mentions your name, what would you like them to remember?

Would you like to make your name super special? You can! First, write down three things God would like you to become. Now create a sentence that includes all three characteristics. Something like, "I have lots of friends because I'm *kind, considerate,* and *helpful*." Now, make it your goal to live up to those attributes. Copy the sentence into your phone or in your school notebook. If you read it several times a day, you'll be reminded of your goals to be more kind, considerate, and helpful. You might be surprised at how quickly your name will come to mean those wonderful things to your friends and to God.

Lord, show us how to create great names
for ourselves that will honor You. Amen.

· Just for Fun ·

Challenge: Can you come up with the name of this famous horse?

- He appeared in more than 80 movies, 101 television show episodes, and won the P.A.T.S.Y. award (an award for animals that's like the Oscars some actors win).

- He was a palomino (gold) with a glossy white mane and tail.

- You may not have seen this horse because he died a long time ago, but you've certainly heard of him.

- He was often called the smartest horse in Hollywood. He could shoot a gun, untie ropes, and was even known to climb stairs at hospitals to visit sick children.

- He was owned by Roy Rogers.

Have you guessed the horse's name?

Yes, it's Trigger! For more information on this amazing horse, type "horse Trigger" on the Internet.

3

Brand Inspection

*You also were included in Christ...marked in him
with a seal, the promised Holy Spirit.*

Ephesians 1:13

A light, warm breeze brushed past me. I glanced at the mare I was buying. She stood tied in the alleyway between the stalls by the large horse arena. Her head hung low as she napped. Today I'd come to pay for her and trailer her home—if the paperwork needed for the sale was in order. The horse trainer, who wore a tall, black cowboy hat, stood next to me. With gnarly hands he held out several sheets of paper.

"I had the veterinarian come out last week for another horse, so I went ahead and had him do the health check on the mare."

I glanced at the health certificate for Dancer. My stomach flip-flopped. *I thought the veterinarian would be here today. Something's wrong.* I'd specifically asked the trainer to wait until I could be here when the doctor examined her. I'd even told him who my veterinarian was. But a different doctor's signature was on the form. *Why would the seller do this? Is he hiding something?* I looked up at him.

A smile spread across his face as he added, "The brand inspection checked out too." I dismissed the uneasy feeling. (A decision I came to regret—I'll tell you about that later.) I turned my attention to the yellow sheet of paper. At the top in bold letters it read "State of Montana Horse Brand Inspection Certificate." The brand inspection paper described what Dancer looked like and that she didn't have any brands on her. In the state of Montana this is important! By law, anytime a person buys a horse, or even crosses a county line with one, they have to have the "brand" paper with them to prove ownership.

I glanced through Dancer's brand papers. They checked out. I was one step closer to writing the check, loading her into the horse trailer, and taking her home.

• Just Between You and Me •

Brands are officially registered with the state where they're used. They help prevent animals from being stolen because brands serve as the owner's signature on the animal. If there is a court case about stolen livestock, the judge will demand that the animals be returned to the person who owns the brand and holds the "brand inspection paper" for that animal. Brand inspections have the final say.

Livestock isn't the only thing that is branded. Did you know that God spiritually "brands" His children? Yes, I wear His brand—and so do you if you've given your life to Jesus. The Bible says that when we believe in Jesus, we're marked with the Holy Spirit. Another version says we're "sealed" with the Holy Spirit. God claims us as His children.

Have you thought of yourself as wearing God's brand? Do you know God loves you—yes, *you!*—so much that He doesn't want you to be stolen from Him?

Lord, thank You for branding us with Your love. Amen.

• Just for Fun •

How many different brands do you think there are in the state of Montana? According to the Montana Department of Livestock, there are approximately 50,000 registered brands. Brands consist of numbers, symbols, and letters arranged in a specific way. They are also assigned a specific location on the animal. My brand is a "Circle 6" that is put on the left thigh on my horses and mules.

Rebecca's brand: "Circle 6."

If you were going to put a brand on your horse, what would it look like? Why not draw your ideas on a sketchpad? Then you can choose one and use it on your school notebooks or in your room. For ideas, you can search the Internet for "livestock brands."

4

Bill of Sale

[God] has purchased us to be his own people.

Ephesians 1:14 NLT

Dancer stood tied in the barn aisle outside of a box stall. A dozen questions thundered through my mind. *Will she like traveling the high, mountain trails? Will she like...?* My hands trembled with excitement as I wrote the check to pay for the red-colored, or sorrel, mare. It was a lot of money, but I thought she was worth it. I handed the check to the trainer, who placed the bill of sale in my hand. Officially she was mine!

I walked over to Dancer and extended my hand in the "horseman's handshake," which meant that I held my hand close to her nose with my palm facing downward. She sniffed it, and then cocked her head side-to-side as she looked at me. I stroked the wide, white blaze on her face. "Today is just the beginning. We've got lots of fun things we're going to do together. Will you be my new best friend?"

"The horseman's handshake."*

• Just Between You and Me •

Some people call me "horse crazy" for wanting to have a horse as my best friend on earth. Well, maybe I am. Do you like horses as much as I do? Each horse has his or her own likes and dislikes, strengths and weaknesses, and unique personality. It takes time to get to know a horse, just like it does when you make a new friend.

My goal with horses and mules is to get to know them so well that I feel like they're part of me. Isn't that the way we feel about our best human friends too? Maybe you know your friend's favorite foods, activities, and stores. Do you have friends you're so close to that you can almost tell what they're thinking?

I have a lot of incredible friends who live all over the world, but my very best friend in the universe is Jesus. Over the years I've learned that He has a personality with likes and dislikes too. Have you ever thought about that? Through reading the Bible, I've learned that He does—just like I do and just like you do. Most of all, I keep discovering how much He loves and cares for me.

Have you considered how much Jesus loves you? The only way we can measure His love is by understanding how much He paid to purchase the "bill of sale" for us. We were very expensive...more costly than the most expensive thing you can think of. Jesus spent everything He had to buy us. He purchased us with His life. He died on the cross as a payment for our sins so that we could know God and live in heaven with Him forever. If we accept Jesus, as our Savior, we can be His best friends forever!

Would you like to become one of His best friends? The first step is to accept Him as your Savior (see the last chapter for more details). Next, you can get to know Him by reading the Bible and spending time talking with Him, which is called prayer, each day. You'll soon begin to understand how priceless you are to Him.

Lord, please show us how to be Your best friend. Amen.

• Just for Fun •

Have you ever read a "bill of sale" form? Make a copy of the one below and fill it out for yourself. Or to download and print a copy of the Bill of Sale, visit http://rebeccaondov.com/For_Horse_Girls_Only.html. Post it on your bedroom wall or the refrigerator as a reminder that you're branded by God and that Jesus bought you with His life. You are loved!

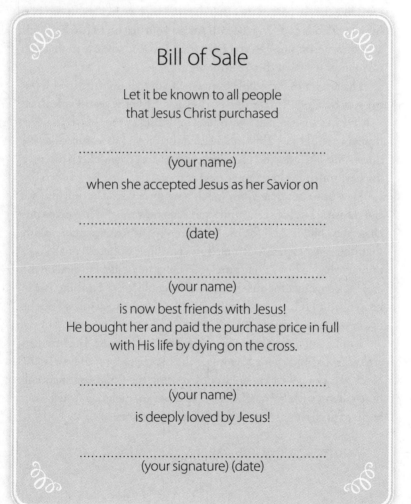

Bill of Sale

Let it be known to all people
that Jesus Christ purchased

....
(your name)

when she accepted Jesus as her Savior on

....
(date)

....
(your name)

is now best friends with Jesus!
He bought her and paid the purchase price in full
with His life by dying on the cross.

....
(your name)

is deeply loved by Jesus!

....
(your signature) (date)

5

Home at Last

Through everything God made, they can clearly see
his invisible qualities—his eternal power and divine nature.
So they have no excuse for not knowing God.

Romans 1:20 NLT

The engine of my red-and-gray diesel truck bogged down as I shifted into first gear and drove through the big green gate. The long, white, gooseneck horse trailer rattled behind as I pulled onto the uneven ground in the horse pasture. After turning off the truck, I hopped out and skipped over to close the gate. From inside the trailer I heard the anxious mare shifting her weight from hoof to hoof. My heart fluttered. I'd just purchased Dancer, and I couldn't wait to unload her. Although I'd worked with hundreds of different horses and mules, I'd never met two that looked exactly alike. I couldn't wait to gawk at the latest addition to my herd.

The back door of the trailer creaked as I pulled it open. Stepping into the trailer, I whispered, "Well, girl, you're home now." From behind the metal divider I saw the tips of the mare's ears swivel to hear my voice and locate where I stood. As I pulled the divider open, she reached her nose toward me. Her long, reddish-gold forelock tumbled over her eyes. Her nostrils quivered and her whiskers wiggled as she inhaled a deep breath of air, which contained all sorts of scents that were new to her. I wondered if she could smell my mule and horses standing in the lower pasture.

I untied her, and the mare stepped lightly behind me as we walked to the back of the trailer. Grasping the side of the doorway, I stepped down onto the grass and moved to the side. The horse poked her head out the trailer and paused. Dancer's head moved left and right as she observed her new home. I leaned against the trailer, admiring the striking contrast between her light, reddish-gold mane and her deep-red body. *A beautiful sorrel,* I thought. A few moments passed and then I tapped the lead rope, asking her to step out of the trailer. She did, but her back right leg had a hitch in it as it reached for the ground. It seemed stiff. I frowned and felt uneasy. I ignored the feeling and asked, "Are you stove-up from being in the trailer, girl? We can walk a few steps to stretch that out." A dozen steps later she seemed to float across the ground.

The afternoon sunlight shimmered off her sleek coat as she plucked individual stems of grass, the muscles rippling smoothly through her neck and back. My mind drifted, marveling at the beauty of God's creation. How did He come up with so many different "models" of horses? Some had shorter, rounder ears. Others had longer backs. Even their colors varied. Some had faint dapples sprinkled throughout their coats. Others looked like God had dipped His paintbrush in black and then outlined the tips of their ears and then dripped it across their bodies.

Suddenly Dancer's ears pricked forward. I heard a faint whinny from the lower pasture. My new mare swung up her head.

"I could stand and stare at you in amazement forever, but it's time for a tour of your new pasture," I told her.

• Just Between You and Me •

Have you noticed how many different sizes and shapes of horses there are, especially in coloring and body features? Only a Being with an enormous imagination could have come up with so many options. Isn't God amazing?

Oftentimes when I'm in a crowd, I think the same thing about people. Each person is so unique. The next time you're in class or at the mall, glance around. Notice that people come in all different shapes, colors, and sizes. Other than a loving God who wanted to create each of us to be individuals, how could that have happened?

The Bible shares the answer to that question by saying that when we look at how marvelously things have been created, we can know for sure that there is a God.

Lord, thank You for proving that You exist through Your marvelous creation. Amen.

• Just for Fun •

If you were to guess the number of horses in the world, how many would you say? According to horsetalk.co.nz, which quotes a study done by the United Nations, in 2006 an estimated 58 million horses were in the world! And to think God created each one to be unique!

6

The Fence

*He is the faithful God who...lavishes his unfailing love
on those who love him and obey his commands.*

Deuteronomy 7:9 NLT

A light breeze fluttered the long strands of my dark-blond hair that had escaped from my braid. Behind me I heard the soft swishing of Dancer's legs pushing through the tall, green grass. It was her first time in this pasture, and I was giving her a tour of her new boundaries. (Whenever I bring new horses into my pasture, I walk them all the way around the fence line. I do that because sometimes when they're turned loose for the first time or if they get startled or scared, they take off running. If they don't know where the fences are, in their panic they might run into them and get injured. To prevent that, I walk the fence with them.)

Dancer's ears tipped toward me as I chattered on. "So, what do you think about your new pasture? There's lots of grass for you to eat. The field is kind of small." My heart sank. My pasture was only five acres. When I worked for outfitters and ranchers, I could turn my horses and mules loose on hundreds, sometimes even thousands of acres of land. I loved watching them romp and play as if they were wild horses. I glanced down the fence line and frowned. The enclosure was so small that the horses couldn't run very far before they had to slow down to turn a corner. It seemed so limiting. Deep inside I felt a little guilty that my animals had to be restrained in such a small space.

As I came to the wooden corner post, I looked over my shoulder.

The mare's head was up, and she was surveying the neighboring pastures. When we got to the "bottom" corner, I paused, turned, and looked into her big brown eyes. "Now this is the important fence. See that highway? Even though it's a mile away, if you went through this side you could get hit by a car."

As I spoke, the words took on new meaning. I gasped in surprise. I'd worked in the wide-open spaces of the mountains so long that I'd begun to believe that fences were bad things. They were too controlling, too confining. But, instead, they actually formed boundaries like a safety net to keep my horses and mules from roaming to places where they could get hurt. The fencing protected them from things they didn't understand, such as cars and trucks speeding down a highway.

Dancer's hooves clopped behind me as I moved forward again. A warm feeling washed over my heart. I twirled the end of the lead rope as I said, "It might not be a very big pasture, but every acre of it is a safety zone for you."

· Just Between You and Me ·

Have you felt that the limits your parents and teachers put on you are too confining or controlling? I have. I used to think that my parents were too strict. And teachers at school? They were too tough. For a long time, it seemed like everywhere I went rules kept me from having fun. But now I realize boundaries are like fences—they're put in place as a safety net.

God's commands are like that too. It's as if He pounds in imaginary fence posts and strings wire around us to keep us safe. He does that because He can see the big picture. Just like I realized the fence kept Dancer safe from the highway, God sees where we could get hurt and sets up a safe boundary. The advice He provides for us through His Word, the Bible, is to keep us from harm because He loves us.

Next time your parents, teachers, or God shows you a "fence line," why not make it a good time to stop and think about how that barrier can protect you from danger you might not fully understand?

Thank You, Lord, for fencing in safety zones
for us through Your Word. Amen.

• Just for Fun •

Have you noticed the different types of fences? When it comes to livestock, it seems like there are a bazillion choices. Everything from wooden posts and rails to metal posts strung with barbed wire, the methods for creating safety zones seem unending. There are even electric fences and "no climb" fences. Why not type "horse fence" into a search engine and see how many kinds you recognize?

If you could choose, what kind of fence would you use to keep your animals safe? Why would you choose that one?

7

My Surprise

Take delight in the LORD, and he will
give you the desires of your heart.

Psalm 37:4

With my finger I traced the white blaze on Dancer's forehead. She closed her eyes as she enjoyed the attention. "Well, girl," I said, "now that you know your boundaries, it's time to meet your pasture pals." As I turned and led the mare toward a gate, my heart flip-flopped. It's always a touchy thing introducing a new horse to a herd. Sometimes personality conflicts flare up for days or weeks. They can even be so bad that the horses never get along and have to be kept in separate pastures...or one of them may need to move to a different home permanently. I was prepared to face that last choice if the trouble was between my elderly horse, Czar, and my new horse.

I'd purchased Czar when he was only a month old. Throughout the years I'd worked from the saddle in the Montana mountains, he'd been my mainstay saddle horse. He'd become my dream horse and had saved my life more than once. We'd become so close that Czar knew what I wanted before I shifted my weight or raised the reins to guide him. He had bonded with me so strongly that he didn't care about other horses when I was around. When we'd ride away from the herd, he never looked back or nickered. When we met unfamiliar horses on the trail, Czar wouldn't even reach out his nose to smell them. He was content to be with me.

In fact, Czar had gotten so attached to me that when he saw me ride another horse, he'd be jealous and pout. He'd squint, lay his ears back, and pucker his lips. Now in his early twenties, Czar's muscles had stiffened with age and all the tough miles we'd covered on the rocky, mountain trails. I couldn't ride him anymore, and I figured he'd earned a nice retirement.

Although I'd purchased Dancer to be my main saddle horse, I didn't want Czar feeling jealous or believing he was being replaced. *God, somehow, someway, would You help him accept Dancer? And let him know that she'll never replace him in my heart?*

My hand trembled as I opened the gate to the little corral that surrounded the barn. I led Dancer through and closed it behind me. The mare's head swung up when she noticed my two horses and mule tied up next to the barn. Her nostrils flared. She whinnied. The others answered. She pranced beside me as I led her next to Czar. I untied him from the post so they could meet, but held onto his lead rope in case I needed to intervene.

The sorrel mare arched her neck. Her long, reddish-gold mane tumbled over her shoulders. Czar stood boldly at attention, his ears pricked toward Dancer. The two horses faced each other, nose to nose, their nostrils quivering. Czar's eyes seemed to brighten. He arched his tail and shifted his shoulders. Suddenly he looked ten years younger! I watched in awe as he tipped his head forward and deeply inhaled her scent. It was like Dancer was wearing an alluring perfume. Almost under his breath he chortled. Lightly, she whickered an answer. I decided they were flirting with each other.

Gently and respectfully the two horses sniffed each other. I stood in awe. For the first time, Czar was interested in another horse when I was around. After decades of ignoring the hundreds of horses he'd been pastured with, he was smitten. I reached up and slipped off their halters. The two of them strolled away, side-by-side. Neither of them squealed or kicked. They seemed to belong together. I nodded my head. *God, that's a miracle. Thank You.*

• Just Between You and Me •

Have you ever felt funny asking God to help you with something that, in the scheme of things, didn't seem very important? Maybe you thought, "God is so big and so busy running the universe, I'm sure He doesn't care about the little things that are happening in my life." But God does. He's the One who put dreams and desires into your heart, and He wants to help you attain them.

Do you need Him to help you with something today? Why not ask for His help right now? Maybe you'll be as surprised as I was when He answers your prayer.

Lord, help us remember that You care about
everything in our lives—large and small. Amen.

• Just for Fun •

How long do horses generally live? A horse who has been well taken care of has a life expectancy of 20 to 30 years. When Czar made his very first, close horse friend (Dancer, his BFF), he was already 28. In human years, that's around 80 years old.

My dream horse, Czar.

8

Only One

I [the Lord God] will give you a shepherd...
He will be your leader, and I will be your God.

Ezekiel 34:23 CEV

A halter hung limply on my shoulder. The buckle jangled as I walked through the pasture toward the large, metal, round pen. Dancer stood in the center. Her ears pricked toward me, and she nickered a greeting. But instead of feeling happy to see her, my stomach churned. Today I was going to turn her loose in the pasture for the first time with my other mare.

A couple days ago when I'd brought Dancer home, I hadn't been concerned about her getting along with my other mare, a tall, large-boned Tennessee walker named Dazzle. After all, Dancer was a smaller horse with what seemed to be a laid-back personality. I was sure she'd easily back down if there was a confrontation just because of the size difference.

Boy, was I wrong. When I led Dancer over to meet the towering black mare who was tied at the hitching rail, the two curiously sniffed noses. Instantly Dancer squinted her eyes, pinned back her ears, and arched her neck. She pawed and squealed and carried on so badly that I hurried to separate them before she could lash out.

For the last several days, I'd kept Dancer inside the metal pen so the two mares could see and smell each other with the security of six-foot-tall metal rails between them. At first Dancer trumpeted challenges. Dazzle tried to be friendly through the fence, but Dancer would nip at her. Clods of dirt flew from their hooves as they raced next to each other, one on each side of the rails. Finally, yesterday, the dust had settled, and I thought they'd worked things out. Or so I hoped.

The gate handle grated as I slid it open and slipped inside the corral. Dancer lumbered next to me and begged for a scratch on her forehead. I stroked her soft fur, slipped the halter in place and buckled it, and then led her into the pasture. I breathed a sigh of relief when I glanced at my black mare, who was standing all the way across the pasture nibbling grass and ignoring us. I held Dancer's lead rope while she cropped grass for a few minutes. The mares chose to ignore each other. Things seemed fine. I lectured Dancer as I slipped off her halter, "The two of you need to get along. Okay?"

I paused and waited several minutes. Nothing negative seemed to be happening, so I turned to walk back to the house. When I got to the top of the small hill, I glanced over my shoulder and noticed that although distance still separated the two horses, they were watching each other. Suddenly Dancer pinned her red ears tightly to her head, gathered herself on her haunches, and spun toward Dazzle. Like a tornado she flew into the black mare's space, seemingly oblivious to the fact that the black horse was nearly twice her size. With hooves and teeth flashing, the whirlwind of sorrel horse kicked and bit the black horse so suddenly and swiftly that Dazzle scurried aside, looking over her shoulder as she wondered what was happening.

I stood dumbfounded. Dancer didn't care that she was a midget next to the other horse. She had the heart of a leader and wasn't going to consider any other possibilities. Instantly she took her stand. I knew that the long-term decision of who would be the herd mare would be decided over several weeks and many confrontations, but today's battle was over instantly. Dancer was the lead mare for now.

• Just Between You and Me •

Just like in a horse herd, there are leaders and followers within groups of people. There's usually one top leader, though, because that's the way God set up things. The leader in your classroom is your teacher. In sports, it's the coach. In a band or choir, it's the director. Even in the group of kids that you hang out with, there's probably one person everyone looks up to or follows.

Who are the leaders in your life?

How do you let God be your ultimate leader and guide?

Lord, show us how to follow You
and let You be our leader. Amen.

• Just for Fun •

In herds of wild horses, the "alpha" or lead mare is the horse that mothers the herd. She's responsible for the herd's overall safety and health. She decides where the herd travels for food and water.

Did you know there are herds of wild horses in the United States today? If you'd like to see photos of the wild horses that roam between Wyoming and Montana, go to www.pryormustangs.org or go to the Internet and type: "Pryor Mountain Wild Mustang Center."

9

Gray Gloomies

[Dear God,] see all these people...
giving freely, willingly—what a joy!

1 Chronicles 29:17 MSG

I busied myself around the house tidying up. I was trying to ignore the thick, dark clouds that had blocked out the sun for the last two weeks. My heart was sad and numb. I'm a sunny kind of a gal, and I don't care for cloudy days—especially day after day after day after day. I swept dust from the coffee table with a feather duster. *God, would You please give me some sunshine?* The gray gloomies had sapped my energy. I didn't even want to go down to the horse pasture. All I really wanted to do was lie down and take a nap—until the sun's smiling face lit up the sky.

A knock on the front door echoed through the living room. I frowned and cocked my head. I lived in the country and wasn't expecting visitors. *Who could that be?* I walked to the front door and pulled it open. On my porch stood two people I'd never seen before. A petite woman held the hand of a little girl, who appeared to be around six years old.

The lady smiled and said, "Hi! My brother just finished building the house below the hill." She pointed down the road. "And this is his daughter, Cassie."

I nodded at both of them. "It's nice to meet you." I stooped low and said, "Hi, Cassie. My name is Rebecca." Shyly the little girl smiled as she shifted her body to hide behind her aunt's leg.

The woman continued. "I came to visit for a couple of days. This morning when I asked Cassie what she'd like to do, she told me she wanted to pet your horses." The bashful girl looked up at me with pleading eyes. The aunt gently caressed her blond hair. "You see, she's been horse crazy since she was born, but she's never had a chance to be around them. Would you be kind enough to let us do that?"

Warmth flooded my heart. I knew how the little girl felt. I'd been the same way when I was her age. I nodded and said, "I'd love to!"

After shrugging on my tan jacket and slipping on my muck boots, the three of us trudged down the hill. Before we reached the bottom, Dazzle, my black Tennessee walker, chortled a hello, closely followed by a whinny from my sorrel mare, Dancer. My ancient horse, Czar, whickered and nodded his head, as if saying, "Hurry up!" Little Girl, my mule, lifted her nose up and brayed loudly: "Heeee haaawww, heeee haaawww."

Cassie's eyes sparkled with anticipation as I opened the gate and shooed them through. The horses and mule were as excited to meet Cassie as she was to meet them. Although they towered over her, the little girl showed no fear. She was in awe. Her dream was coming true.

My friendly critters stretched their necks and gently snuffled her from head to toe. Then Czar lowered his head to her waist level and held it there, begging for her attention. Tentatively she stroked the white star on his forehead. Czar ate it up. Over the next half hour I showed Cassie and her aunt where the animals loved to be scratched. I chattered about each horse and my mule.

When it was time for her to go, a smile beamed across Cassie's face. She looked up at me with adoration. I could see the sunshine of Jesus' love in her eyes. By letting her pet the critters, I'd given her a gift she'd cherish the rest of her life. Although the weather was still dark and blustery when I climbed the hill behind the little girl and her aunt, my heart was skipping with joy. The gray gloomies had been chased out as soon as I'd taken my eyes off me and focused on helping someone else.

• Just Between You and Me •

Have you noticed that when you think about yourself a lot, the gray gloomies dribble into your heart and make you sad, or mad, or just plain grumpy? That's because God doesn't want us to always think about ourselves. He created us to be like Him, and He loves to give of Himself.

Have you noticed that when you think about doing things for others, your heart feels happy? That's because you're displaying God's personality.

Knowing this, what can you do to cheer yourself up the next time you feel sad or grumpy?

Lord, help us see what we can do for the people
around us. Then remind us to do it. Amen.

• Just for Fun •

Do you know where horses like to be scratched? Over the years, I've discovered one universal spot horses and mules loved to be scratched or rubbed. It's on the side of their neck, right where it joins with the chest and shoulders.

Rebecca scratching one of Dazzle's favorite spots.*

10

Better Than Best Friends

Jesus replied: "If anyone loves me, they will obey me.
Then my Father will love them, and
we will come to them and live in them."

John 14:23 CEV

I pushed the water tank for livestock on its side. Splash! The remaining water rushed over the dry ground. Instantly Czar, my bay gelding, and Dancer lifted their heads from where they were eating grass and wandered over. Ever since I'd brought Dancer home, the two had been inseparable. I watched them walk side-by-side toward me. *They're even in step with each other!*

With a big brush, I scrubbed out the tank. Suddenly I felt something warm on my back. I glanced up, and both Czar and Dancer were standing behind me watching my every move. "You two look like someone glued you together," I commented.

They batted their long eyelashes at me.

I flipped the tank upright and turned on the water spigot full force. The water sprayed into the tank. After it rose a couple inches, the two horses stepped over to take a look. Their movements matched perfectly. It was almost as if one was a mirror reflection of the other. They lowered their heads into the stock tank at the exact same moment. They drew water into their mouths with little sucking noises and even seemed to swallow at precisely the same time.

I tucked a loose strand of my blond hair behind my ear and watched with awe as they lifted their heads in sync, turned together, and strolled to the 50-pound square block of salt. With the same smooth motions, they lowered their heads together, looking eye to-eye as they licked the salt. I'd never seen anything like it. It was as if they'd become one horse.

Czar was so in love with Dancer that he wouldn't leave her side. And obviously the sorrel mare felt the same way about him. They'd become better than best friends. An interesting thought drifted through my mind. *I have wonderful friends, but I would love to have a "one in a million" friend like that.*

Instantly I heard in my spirit Jesus' still small voice: "You have Me."

• Just Between You and Me •

Do you have a really close friend you pal around with? Someone who enjoys doing the same types of things you do? God created us to need each other, and He created gals to need gal friends. We're all about relationships. We love to share our feelings, secret thoughts, and dreams.

Through the years I've made incredible gal friends, but the best friend I've ever had is Jesus. I'm still amazed that when we ask Jesus to be our Savior, He comes and lives in our hearts. From that moment on, we're never alone! Jesus is always living inside us. He's everywhere we go. He sees everything we do. He hears and understands every thought we think. And the best part is He wants to be "better than our best friends too."

Lord, help us make and be wonderful friends with other gals and with You. Amen.

• Just for Fun •

Horses are very social animals, so they prefer to live together in herds. Oftentimes after a horse has lived within a herd for a while, he or she hangs out with the same horse, and they become best friends. Telltale signs of friendships are when you see them grooming each other, swatting flies off each other with their tails, and taking afternoon naps together. Although I've watched hundreds of horses, I've never seen two horses be "better than best friends" like Czar and Dancer.

11

The Bully

Don't be intimidated by all this bully talk.

Matthew 10:31 MSG

I dabbed the bleeding wound on Dazzle's back with disinfectant. The black mare seemed to grit her teeth in pain as she watched me with her soft and kind eyes. I was sure she knew I was helping her. I winced when I looked at the long strip where the hide was missing. It ran from Dazzle's withers to her tail, about an inch wide, along the whole top of her back.

My emotions boiled. I squinted when I glanced at the culprit—Dancer. I'd only owned her a couple weeks. Although toward humans she was kind and gentle, when she got around Dazzle the pint-sized sorrel horse would morph into a wild storm, kicking and squealing. If Dazzle even glanced at the other mare, World War III would break out. Today Dancer had cornered the black mare in the barn and lashed out with her front hooves, scalping a strip of hide.

I knew there was only room for one mare to be in charge, but this was ridiculous. Dancer wasn't being a good leader. She'd turned into a bully. And Dazzle refused to back down, although she never fought back. *Would they ever learn to get along? Do I need to separate them?* My pasture wasn't set up for that. I couldn't keep them apart forever. *Do I need to sell Dancer?* My heart ached at the thought. Czar had fallen head-over-heels in love with her. *I can't take her away from him.* Besides, I'd purchased her as a saddle horse, and horseback riding season was just starting. *Would I be able to sell her and find another*

41

horse before the summer was over? What am I going to do? I continued to ponder the problem as I finished doctoring Dazzle.

Over the next few days I kept a close eye on the two mares. As long as the big, black horse faded into the background, the pasture seemed peaceful. Then I noticed something that made me angrier. That little red mare wasn't letting Dazzle get near the other horses or my mule. She'd stolen Dazzle's friends away from her. Day after day Dazzle calmly stood on the outside looking in. My heart ached for her. She didn't have a mean bone in her body. The herd had been hers before I introduced the bully into the mix. *Do I need to get rid of that new horse?* I waited and watched. The relationship between the two horses smoldered.

Days later I tossed hay into the feeder. The sorrel mare bobbed her head at the other horses as if to say, "This is my feed!" Then she bellied up to the feeder to be first. Dazzle patiently waited for me to toss hay in the other feeder for her. When I did, she gently nudged me, asking for some attention. As I stroked her fur, she watched me with her kind, soft eyes. Respect washed over me. Throughout all the bullying and the injury, my black horse hadn't changed. She'd stood at a distance, but she hadn't been intimidated. She didn't quake with fear, and she didn't bully Dancer back. Dazzle never started fights. She didn't lash out in anger or become mean. She was as steady as a rock. No matter what happened on the outside, she seemed to know who she was on the inside.

Only time would tell if I would keep the little red tornado, but I knew Dazzle would be with me as long as she lived.

• Just Between You and Me •

Have you ever been bullied? I was. My school years were painful. I wore eye glasses that constantly slipped down my small, Norwegian, ski-jump-like nose. They were so thick that my depth-perception was off a little bit, so when I played sports and tried to catch the ball, my eyesight would tell my brain the wrong information. I fumbled the ball a lot, knocked it out of bounds, and painfully jammed the ends of my fingers.

The pain and embarrassment weren't the worst part either. The other kids' snickers and cutting words scalped me. After hearing the taunts time and again, I started to believe there was something wrong with me. The facts were clear. When teams were chosen to play kick-ball or soccer, I was always the last person standing...the only one waiting to be chosen. I figured out I must be a loser.

Back then, I wish I'd had a big black horse like Dazzle to show me how to stay steady. She would've helped me not let those ugly words take root in my heart. She would've been a model for how to *not* lash out or become angry. No matter what was happening on the outside, Dazzle would have shown me that I was valuable, and steady, and able to stand my ground calmly.

Rebecca and Dazzle.*

It's taken years to wash those nasty words from my heart. I finally realized that what I believe about myself is my choice. Nobody can "make me feel" a certain way. What I choose to think determines what I feel. I can choose to not let words hurt me. I can choose to not let bullying make me mad. However, I'm not saying you should let yourself be bullied. If you are being bullied, find someone who can help you without resorting to the same type of behavior. Talk to your parents or your school counselor for options.

I've found some Bible verses that help remind me who I am in Christ, and I think about them often. One of my favorites is: "GOD chose you out of all the people on Earth as his cherished personal treasure" (Deuteronomy 14:2 MSG). Do you think of yourself as God's cherished and personal treasure? I hope so!

So, what are you going to choose to believe about yourself today?

Lord, help us always look at ourselves through
Your eyes of love. Amen.

• Just for Fun •

I was extremely upset with Dancer for the way she acted toward Dazzle. Years later, when I was reading about wild horse behavior, I discovered that Dancer had been acting out of instinct. In a wild herd, when one mare decides she'll be the alpha or top mare, she'll drive out any horse that refuses to acknowledge or follow her leadership.

In wild herds, being driven out can be a death sentence for the horse. A lone horse doesn't have the herd to protect him or her. Horses stay safe from mountain lions, grizzly bears, and wolves by staying in a group and facing the danger together. Sometimes the horses that were driven out are allowed to rejoin the herd, but they must accept and live under the herd mare's authority.

12

The Bubble Bath

Even before time began God planned for
Christ Jesus to show kindness to us.

2 Timothy 1:9 CEV

The shampoo bottle sputtered. I squeezed it, and globbed some liquid onto the large sponge in six-year-old Cassie's hand. A big grin wiggled across her face. A few days ago I'd invited Cassie, a six-year-old neighbor girl, over for a horsey bubble-bath party. She was horse-crazy and Dazzle loved bubble baths, so it was a perfect fit. My soaking wet black Tennessee walker stood next to us on my asphalt driveway just outside the large, opened garage door. I'd sprayed her down with warm water, and dirty brown water was dripping off her belly and running down her tail, which was so long that it swept the ground. The dribbling water reminded me of the tears that had run down my face earlier that morning. A while ago, my best friend had moved. Today was one of those days that my heart ached because I missed her. *God, I need a woman friend, someone with whom I can share my thoughts and dreams. Will you please mend my heart?*

I faked a smile and shook a blob of shampoo onto my sponge. I looked at Cassie. "Okay, let's soap Dazzle up starting at the top of her neck."

Cassie stood on her tippy-toes. Using the sponge, she gently rubbed the soap into Dazzle's wet fur. Suddenly, the mare dropped her head to within a couple feet of the ground. Alarmed, the little girl stopped and stepped back. "Does she like this?" she asked worriedly.

Dazzle all soaped up.*

Smearing more soap onto the horse's neck, I nodded. "She loves it. That's why she lowered her head—so you can reach."

"Really?" She smiled, and her little fingers quickly scrubbed some more.

Dazzle closed her eyes and sighed with joy.

"See how she's relaxing, Cassie? She thinks you're giving her a massage. Dazzle loves the attention. She's all girl. She'd probably like it if we painted her hooves with sparkly fingernail polish."

Cassie giggled as she crafted the soap into big bubbles.

My heart got lighter as Cassie and I chatted about our dreams of horses and riding.

Twenty minutes and one bottle of shampoo later, my black horse wore a coat of white bubbles. I scampered through the garage and into the laundry room in my house to turn on the warm water so we could hose off the bubbles. Soon Dazzle's coat gleamed bluish-black as the sun glistened off individual strands of hair.

Cassie stepped back and admired the horse. "She's pretty when she's clean." Then the little girl's face turned sour, as if something was wrong. "How do horses get clean if people don't give them bubble baths?"

I grinned. "That's why God sends the rain—to wash the dirt away. He thought of everything when He planned out the world." My mind took the thought another step. *He even sent a horse-crazy girl to a neighbor's place to ease the pain of the neighbor's best friend moving away.*

Dazzle laughing about her bath.*

• Just Between You and Me •

Have you had a day when everything worked out so well that it seemed like God must have planned the whole thing? The amazing thing is that He did.

Even though Cassie was so much younger than I was, over the next few years we developed a fun friendship. And God brought other friends into my life too, so my heart quit aching. But more importantly, I saw how God didn't want my heart to be sad, so He sent friends to brighten my days. He knew what I needed before I did and arranged everything. The great part is that He'll do the same for you.

Lord, thank You for planning in advance so many
good things for us. Amen.

• Just for Fun •

How often does a horse need a bath? That depends on the horse and what you're using him (or her) for. If it's a show horse, you'll be bathing him before every competition. If it's a horse who lives outside in a pasture, it's better to not give them very many baths. Soap removes the natural oils in a horse's coat, and those oils help the horse be somewhat waterproof during wet weather.

Oh, and there are companies that really make sparkly "fingernail polish" for horses. Type "Hoof polish" on the Internet to check it out.

13

Smoke!

Do not be discouraged.

Deuteronomy 1:21

Dancer stood tied to the hitching post and closed her eyes as I groomed her with light brush strokes. The summer sun lulled her into a mid-morning nap. I was excited because today was the first day I'd be able to ride her since I'd purchased her. I glanced at a mountain a few miles north of my home. A wide, black plume of smoke rose from the backside where a forest fire had blown up.

Over the last few weeks the winds had funneled blankets of thick smoke into the valley where I lived. More than anything, I wanted to go horseback riding, but I didn't want to breathe the smoke or have Dancer inhale too much smoke during a workout, so we'd stayed home. The worst part was that the fire kept growing. Every day the smoke was thicker than the day before. But this morning the air was clear. *Maybe I can sneak in a ride before the air turns gray.*

I tossed a saddle blanket and saddle on Dancer's back and tightened the cinch. When I did, she gave a deep, raspy cough. I stopped. "Girl, are you okay?" Dancer lowered her head, stretched her neck, and coughed again. The sorrel turned her head and looked at me. Tears welled in the corner of her eyes. I sighed. "Okay, so it's not very smoky today, but it's still bothering you, isn't it?" My heart sank as I thought about my options. I could ride her and pretend everything was okay, but that wouldn't be fair to Dancer. Obviously her lungs were sore from the smoke. I could unsaddle her and put her back in the pasture. My mind and heart argued with me. *But I bought her to ride...not to stand around in a pasture.*

I groaned as I made the right choice and stripped the saddle off. I hung it on the saddle rack and put the saddle blanket in its spot. I turned Dancer loose. The rest of the week I grew more discouraged as the fire grew larger. Morning and night when I went down to feed the horses, they coughed and wheezed. Some days the smoke was so thick I could barely see a block away. Tears from my animals' eyes ran all the way down their faces and dripped off their chins. I felt so badly for them...and all the animals in our valley. My heart ached when I looked at my saddle that was growing dusty from hanging on the rack.

After weeks and weeks of the same old thing, the newspapers announced that it was dangerous to breathe the smoke. I phoned a friend who lived on the other side of the mountains and asked if I could move my horses and mule into her pasture for a while. She said sure. With a heavy heart because I'd miss them, I loaded them into the trailer and hauled them over there. On the drive, my thoughts ranted about how horrible the fire was and how it was ruining my summer. It was destroying my dream of riding my new horse in the wilderness area. By the time the tires on my truck crunched down Dena's gravel driveway, I was sad and discouraged.

Dancer coughed and hacked while I unloaded her. With a scowling voice I said to Dena, "There goes my summer."

Dena's eyes twinkled with friendliness and optimism. "But, Rebecca, you've got next year."

Humbled, I dropped my gaze to the ground and led Dancer into a wooden corral. Dena was right. I'd been wasting my life by thinking about how my dream wasn't coming true. I'd become discouraged because I viewed myself as being picked on by events that were beyond my control. But the world wasn't ending. Nor was the dream God had given me. I could cheer myself up by looking at the blessings God had given me today and looking forward to riding next year. I could even focus on how blessed I was to have a friend who would share her pasture. It was my choice what I wanted to think about. That day I changed my thought pattern.

• Just Between You and Me •

Have you been discouraged when you didn't get what you wanted? Or when something you planned didn't turn out the way you wanted? What kind of thoughts went through your mind? Did you get angry and focus on everything that went wrong? That's easy to do, but is that the way God wants us to choose?

When I think about people who could have gotten discouraged because they didn't get what they wanted, I think about Joshua. In the Bible, in the book of Numbers, chapters 13 and 14, is the story about God commanding the Israelites to go into the Promised Land. (Why not read Numbers 13 and 14 right now?) Moses sent 12 spies into the land to check things out. Everyone came back with bad and discouraging reports—that is, everyone except Joshua and Caleb (Numbers 13:26-30; 14:6-9). Of the 12 spies, only the two of them believed God's dream for Israel and that God would give them victory over the people who lived there. But the people of Israel didn't believe, so they disobeyed God. Although God forgave them, He also said that because the Israelites treated Him with contempt, they would wander the desert until the ones who refused to believe died. After they died, their children, along with Joshua and Caleb, got to go into the Promised Land (Numbers 14:20-38).

Joshua didn't get to do what he wanted for 40 years. He had to wander in the desert too. He could have become bitter and angry at the people around him who had caused the delay. But, instead, he chose to listen to God, to be strong and courageous, and to not be discouraged. God made Joshua Moses' successor as leader of the Israelites because Joshua was faithful and followed God. What a wonderful reward Joshua received for choosing to believe God and focus on His blessings.

Would you like to be rewarded for being faithful to God? The key is to believe God, learn and meditate (think about) His promises and truths in the Bible, and follow His wisdom.

The next time you feel discouraged, what would be a good way to move forward? Even small steps are okay. For instance, a smile because God is with you might be a great way to start.

Lord, when we become sad and discouraged, open our eyes so we can see the blessings You've given us. Amen.

• Just for Fun •

Are you wondering if my horses and mule recovered from inhaling the awful forest fire smoke? They did, but it took almost a year before they quit coughing and wheezing. Forest fires, especially in the Western United States, have become more common in the last 20 years. It's a hot topic of discussion. Some people believe forest fires are harmful and should be put out as soon as possible. Others believe forest fires are good for the land.

Why don't you look up and read about forest fires? Then make a list of three good things and three bad things about them.

14

The Radio

Shout for joy to the Lord, all the earth,
burst into jubilant song with music.

Psalm 98:4

I'd just walked from the horse trailer and into the garage when I heard "Bam! Bam! Bam!" Dancer, who was tied inside the horse trailer, was repeatedly striking the wall with her hoof. I poked my head out the garage door and yelled, "Stop that!" But instead of stopping, she pounded against the wall like a jackhammer. Frustrated, I threw my hands up and walked back to the trailer.

Today I was hauling her to the veterinarian clinic for a routine checkup. Dancer didn't like loading or being in the trailer. I'd worked with her on it, but some days went more smoothly than others. Because I didn't want to be late to the appointment, I'd allowed an extra hour to load her just in case she balked. But she didn't. She stepped right in today. Even though I was now ahead of schedule, I didn't dare unload her because she might not load nicely again. I reasoned, *It won't hurt her to wait in the trailer.*

The window to her stall in the horse trailer was down. Her ears pricked forward as I walked toward her. She whinnied loudly and shook her head as if saying, "Let's get going."

I reached through the window and stroked her forehead. I cooed, "I know you're nervous, girl, but nothing will hurt you. It's a big, comfortable trailer." Dancer's head relaxed as I patted her neck. "Okay, I'm going to get some stuff done in the house. You can take a nap."

But as soon as I walked out of sight, that little red horse sounded like an elephant on a destruction crew. *She'd better not be putting any dents in the trailer!* I thought. I heard her smacking the walls, and her voice was trumpeting like bugle blasts calling troops to battle. I peeked out the window and saw the trailer rocking from side to side. I squinted. *Okay, she does this every time because she doesn't want to be alone. I've got five bazillion things to do, so I don't have the time or patience to stand next to the trailer and babysit her. Besides, she has to learn to stand in the trailer sometime.* I paused. *God, what do I do?* I asked as I leaned my back against the garage door and sighed. Suddenly my glance noticed my workbench...and a boom box. "That's it! A radio!"

I scooped up the radio, plugged it into an outside outlet, and tuned it to K-LOVE, a favorite Christian station. As the notes of a peaceful song drifted through the air, Dancer paused. I watched through the trailer window as she cocked her head. She stared toward the radio, as if trying to figure out what it was.

Dancer

I giggled. In my imagination I could see Dancer trying to figure out how somebody stuffed all those people—and a band—into that tiny box. By the time the station switched to a new song with another light melody, her whole body had relaxed as the rhythm of the music soothed her soul. *Wow! Everything's changed. It's like God wrapped His arms of peace around her so she doesn't feel like she's alone.*

I quietly slipped into the house. Although I carefully listened and kept glancing out the window, I never heard a peep out of the mare or saw the trailer rocking. An hour later when I went outside, Dancer was still calmly listening to the music. K-LOVE, had gained another fan—a four-footed one. I marveled at God's solution. Who would have thought of turning on a radio for a horse?

• Just Between You and Me •

Have you noticed that music can easily change your mood? On dark, gloomy days, I like to turn on jazzy music or sing silly songs to lighten my heart. Oftentimes when I'm writing, I play a CD with nature sounds.

Have you ever been shopping in the mall or a store and heard songs with loud, banging music? Maybe they even had words with bad meanings? Some may have sounded mean or scary. When I hear them, they trouble my heart. I get edgy and cranky. Has that ever happened to you? That's because music sets the atmosphere.

Did you know there are a couple stories in the Bible that talk about this same thing? Does that surprise you? When King Saul didn't feel well or he was upset, he would call for David. David would play his harp and sing, and King Saul would soon feel better. The Bible says the evil spirit tormenting Saul would go away (1 Samuel 16:23 CEV).

In another story, God's prophet Elisha asked for someone to play the harp. When the harpist played, God gave Elisha special wisdom to share (2 Kings 3:15). Throughout the book of Psalms, we're encouraged to worship God with music. It's because music and the words affect our whole being and set the atmosphere of peace and love.

So the next time you're sad or angry, you could turn on some fun music, such as your favorite Christian radio station, and change the atmosphere from a sad one to a happy one with the push of a button. What do you think?

Lord, show us how to create an atmosphere
of happiness and peace around us. Amen.

• Just for Fun •

Did you know that oftentimes people play music in horse arenas when they ride and train? The music helps the rider and the horse establish a rhythm and keep in sync with each other. Trainers have been using music for centuries. You might want to check out "The Pony Cafe" on Facebook.

15

Mud Works!

*We take captive every thought to
make it obedient to Christ.*

2 Corinthians 10:5

The golden leaves on the aspen trees rattled in the hot and dry September breeze. A swarm of flies followed me as I tossed hay into the feeders for the horses. Bzzz...bzzz. *How irritating!* One landed in my hair, and I swatted at it. It spiraled around and flew over to land on Dazzle. She stomped her feet and swatted her tail at the pesky critters. Even though I'd sprayed the horses with fly spray, the winged creatures didn't seem to notice. They'd set their sights on having some juicy horseflesh for dinner. I shook my head. *I wish there was something more I could do for my horses and mule, but what?*

I waved my hand in front of my face to shoo the flies away. I glanced at the stock water tank. Momentarily sidetracked, I thought, *It wouldn't hurt to dump it and put in fresh water.* I grasped the side and heaved. The metal tank banged as it flipped on its side. Splash! A wave of water rolled across the dirt. I grabbed a big yellow brush and scrubbed the sides to clean it out.

My thoughts drifted to a get-together I'd been at the day before with friends. We'd laughed and had fun, but after I'd driven away, pesky thoughts buzzed through my mind. And they hadn't stopped. I chewed on my lip and brooded. *The other gals were all dressed up, and I'd only worn my jeans. Maybe I should have dressed up too.* I glanced down. My hands were rough from working outside, and my fingernails were chipped. *I hope they didn't notice my horsey-looking hands.* On and on thoughts like those droned as thick as the swarm of flies around me. Now it was a day later, and instead of feeling better, my little fears had grown into giant horseflies.

Dazzle dawdled over to the puddle where I'd dumped the water out of the stock tank. Flies covered her body. She switched her tail and pawed the mud.

I frowned. "What are you doing?"

The big horse gathered all four of her feet together and plopped down. She rolled onto her back. With her feet in the air she wiggled as if scratching her back. She rubbed her neck and face on the ground until she was coated with mud. Groaning, she heaved to her feet. Instead of shaking off the gooey mud, she walked to the feeder and nibbled on strands of hay.

She looked disgusting with globs of mud sticking to her fur. But a couple minutes later I noticed there wasn't a fly on her. I laughed out loud. "That's brilliant, Dazzle! You just encased yourself in mud to protect yourself from the flies!"

No sooner had I said that when God's still small voice whispered to my spirit, "You can do the same thing. By hiding in Me, you can protect yourself from those pesky thoughts that are bugging you." I hadn't thought of it that way. When self-doubt swirled through my mind, I could choose to not think about them. Instead, I could focus my thoughts on how much God loves me just as I am.

• Just Between You and Me •

Have you had pesky thoughts bug you? Thoughts about how you're not good enough? Or smart enough? Or pretty enough? Try as we might, we never will be "enough" or have "enough." There will always be a nicer dress we could have worn, and a more flattering hair style. There's always something we could have said or done better. It's good to consider those things and work to improve them to the best of our ability. But there's a point when we have to stop those self-defeating thoughts and replace them with thoughts of how much God loves us just as we are.

Lord, thank You for loving us despite our broken fingernails and messy hair. Amen.

• Just for Fun •

Have you noticed how horses keep flies off each other? Oftentimes on hot afternoons, if you look into a pasture you'll see two horses standing side-by-side but facing opposite directions. When they swish their tails, they brush across the other horse's face and swat the flies away. Pretty ingenious, don't you think?

16

A Grateful Heart

*It is wonderful to be grateful and to
sing your praises, LORD Most High!*

Psalm 92:1 CEV

Sleet pelted me in the face. I pulled my wool cap down and rounded
my shoulders like a turtle's shell to shelter my neck from the Novem-
ber storm. *I hate this season of the year. By the time I finish feeding the
horses and mule, I'll be soaked.* My animals stood huddled together
under the overhang of the barn, dripping wet and shivering. They
watched me slosh through the mud and duck into the barn. My ugly
attitude oozed out of me as I swept the slush off the shoulders of my
slicker. *I hate being cold!*

I pulled the pocketknife out of its belt clip and reached up to cut
the twine on a bale of hay in the haystack. When I did, several drops
of icy water rolled down my back. I shivered. *Why do I live in the
north? I should just pack my bags and move!* I loaded the little green
wagon with several flakes of alfalfa hay. After scooping some grain
into a white, five-gallon bucket, I set it inside the wagon too.

The wagon bumped behind me as I dragged it through the mud.
Grumpily I tossed hay into Czar and Dancer's feeder, along with a
scoop of grain for each. The two of them charged up to their feeders
and gobbled the grain. As I pulled the wagon toward the other feeder,
I mumbled under my breath, "I bet you guys hate this soggy and nasty
weather too!" Patiently Dazzle and Little Girl waited for me to toss
hay into their feeder and dish out their scoops of grain.

For a moment I rested my arm on Dazzle's back and listened to the horses munching. Out of the corner of my eye, I noticed my red mare bobbing her head. Standing next to the feeder, she'd tipped her head up and put her nose in the air. Then she'd lifted her top lip up so that her white teeth showed. Over and over she waved her head into the sky and waggled her lip. I giggled. It was her way of saying "Thank you" for the grain. She always made sure I saw her.

I walked toward her. "Dancer, you're a silly girl." She lowered her head and batted her red eyelashes at me. A cold breeze gusted, and I pulled the wool scarf tucked around my neck a little higher and tighter. Dancer nuzzled me when I stepped next to her. *How can you stand there hungry, soaking wet, and shivering in the cold, and yet still remember to thank me?* Then I heard God's voice in my spirit. "You could take a lesson from her."

The words stabbed my heart. It was true. Ever since I'd rolled out of bed that morning I'd whined and complained. About the weather. About where I lived. About having to go out in the miserable rain. Instead, I could have been grateful—grateful that I had horses and a mule to feed no matter what the weather was like. Grateful that I had a job to earn the money to buy hay and grain. Grateful I had a barn where they could be sheltered from the worst of the storm.

God used my silly red horse to remind me to count my blessings even when I was miserable in the midst of a storm.

• Just Between You and Me •

Have you ever had a day when it seemed like everything went wrong at school or at home? In your mind did you make a list of everything bad that happened? Did you concentrate on the icky stuff? How did you feel?

When I only think about the bad, I get grumpy and mad at the world. But God showed me that the problem wasn't about what was happening to me. The problem was how I was choosing to respond.

As soon as I quit dwelling on the icky thoughts and remembered what God had done for me, my whole day improved.

Will you try this the next time you're having a bad day? What do you think will happen?

Lord, help us to always look for Your blessings.
Teach us to focus on them...and You. Amen.

• Just for Fun •

Have you ever seen a horse or mule flip their top lip up? It's one of the funniest things to watch. Horses and mules communicate through body language. They learn it from their mothers, other horses, and from their friendships with humans. I've often wondered where Dancer learned to do it. Was it from her mother? I'll never know, but with her the meaning is always clear. She's saying, "Thank you."

Did you know that some of the most famous horse trainers have studied the body language of horses so they can "talk" to their horses through gestures and motions. For fun, type in "horse body language" on the Internet and see what comes up.

17

Smile!

*I always want to be as brave as I am now
and bring honor to Christ.*

Philippians 1:20 CEV

A blustery wind rocked my little writing studio, which was perched on a slope in my horse pasture. Thick snow blew sideways and pelted the windows as I typed an email. I hovered the computer mouse over the "send" button and then leaned back in my chair and sighed. I was about to post my first homework assignment for an online class so the other classmates could review it. I was in the process of writing a story for a children's movie. It seemed like most of the other folks in the class were writing horror and shoot-'em-up adult stories. I didn't want to write about violence. I wanted to write something that I would be excited to have Jesus read. I rubbed my forehead. *Will my classmates think my idea is too simple? What will the teacher think because I shared my faith in Jesus in the story?*

Stones rattled down the hill next to my studio. The horses and Little Girl, my brown mule, walked down the steep trail, their hooves knocking some rocks loose. They paused at the window and looked in. Snow was caked on them so thickly that they looked like huge snowmen. Chunks fell off their backs like avalanches as they continued their march into the pasture below. *So much for the weather report this morning. Wrong again. They'd said the weather would be nice.* Even my critters' eyelashes were coated with white flakes. I chuckled. *The snow on their coats tells the whole story. Maybe I should take a picture of Little*

Girl and call her "The Montana Weather Mule"? She's better at forecasting the weather than the weatherman.

I grabbed my camera off the desk, slipped into my down jacket, and tugged on my hat and mittens. My muck boots squeaked through the snow. Little Girl stood huddled next to the horses by the barn. Mules typically grow thicker fur in the winter than horses do. Her winter coat was about four inches long, so the snow piled on her the deepest. Even her whiskers glistened with frosty snowflakes. I pulled the camera out of my pocket and turned it on. It hummed as the lens moved into place. Little Girl squinted suspiciously at the noise. Centering her in the viewfinder, I exclaimed, "Smile!" and pushed the button. The camera clicked and then the flash went off.

Little Girl, "The Montana Weather Mule"

Little Girl's eyes widened. She spun halfway around and scooted across the pasture.

"Little Girl! I'm so sorry. I forgot to turn off the flash." I pushed my way through the snow to her side. "Little Girl, it's okay. I won't do it again. I'm sorry."

She paused, her snowy ears swiveling and her nostrils flaring. She stared and snorted at the camera in my hand.

I held it toward her so she could smell it. She immediately jumped back like something had bitten her. She turned and dashed away again.

I whined as I shuffled behind her. "Little Girl, there's nothing to be afraid of. Don't be so silly! The camera is harmless. It won't hurt you. C'mon, don't be a wimp. All you have to do is be brave and smile."

My insides shriveled as the words "be brave and smile" echoed through my mind. How could I tell her that when I'd been too wimpy to turn in a homework assignment? I pocketed the camera.

Little Girl arched her neck and eyed me. I stepped toward her. "Okay, girl, no more cameras today. Being brave is something we're both going to have to work on."

• Just Between You and Me •

Have you noticed that it's always easier to tell someone else to be brave? When it comes to us, we'd rather hide, especially when we're trying to avoid sharing something very personal. For instance, when we're asked to do things that reveal our Christian faith we can get shy.

I'd like to say that when you get older it gets easier, but it doesn't. Taking a stand for Jesus requires bravery and courage no matter how old we are. It means doing what is right no matter what could happen.

Usually when we take a stand for something, the people around us respect us for it even if they don't agree with the cause or issue. Sometimes our fears are realized, but knowing we did the right thing helps. In other situations, we might discover that our fear was based on very little in the first place, just like Little Girl's fear of the camera. That's what I discovered too. Later that day I emailed my homework assignment to the entire class. During the next 10 weeks, my classmates gave me suggestions on how to develop my story. My teacher helped too. It truly had been a silly fear.

*Lord, show us how to be brave and stand up
to our fears with Your courage. Amen.*

• Just for Fun •

Mules are notorious for being scaredy-cats. When they see or hear new or unusual things, they have to check it out before moving forward. They're so smart that they won't do something that might hurt them. That's how the expression "stubborn as a mule" got started.

The trick to training them is to be smarter than they are. Break down the goal into very small steps. Teach them one at a time and in ways that let the mules think it was their idea. Although it takes longer, once they get it they usually never forget.

18

Clop, Clop, Clop, Clump

*Jesus and the people he makes holy
all belong to the same family.*

Hebrews 2:11 CEV

Spring had finally come to the mountains. Snow was melting off the tall peaks, and the buds on the cottonwood trees were popping open into bright green leaves. The afternoon sun warmed my arms as I rode down the dirt road on my way home. It was my first horseback ride of the season. And it was one of my first rides on Dancer, the sorrel mare I'd bought nearly a year ago. I hadn't been able to ride her last summer because the smoke from the forest fires was so thick and dangerous to breathe.

Dancer picked up her pace as we neared home. I noticed that instead of a smooth and even walk, it felt like her right hind leg had a "hitch" in it. By the time I reined her to a stop next to my mailbox, she was dragging the foot just a little. Her walk even sounded odd. Instead of "clop, clop, clop, clop," it was "clop, clop, clop, clump."

I swung my leg over the saddle and dismounted. I stood next to her head and patted her neck. "Did you twist your foot on a rock today?" While holding the reins, I reached down and asked her to pick up her hind leg. She did, and I checked the hoof for a rock or some kind of injury. Nothing seemed odd. I shrugged. "I'll check again in the morning, girl. I bet you'll be okay."

I stepped to my mailbox and pulled out a stack of papers. I spied the address on the corner of a large envelope. The return address read

"TWHBEA." I looked at Dancer. "Yes! It's your Tennessee Walking Horse registration papers!" My heart thumped as I ripped open the envelope. It had been a hard decision whether to register her. There was a fee, and at that point I hadn't been sure if I'd be keeping her. When I first purchased her and brought her home, she'd been kind and gentle—until she got around my black mare. Then Dancer had morphed into a blur of teeth and striking hooves. One time she even scalped a strip of hide off of the black mare's back. It took months, but finally she left the other mare alone. That's when I mailed in Dancer's registration papers.

I pulled out several folded sheets. The letter said I'd filled out an old form, so they needed me to fill out the new form. I also needed to have the previous owner sign them. No big deal. *Okay, I'll call him tomorrow.* I had no idea what I was going to discover.

I tucked the mail in my back pocket and stroked Dancer's neck. "We're going to have so much fun riding this summer." Little did I know that would *never* happen.

• Just Between You and Me •

Did you know that a horse's registration papers are a form of birth certificate? They tell who the horse's mother (dam), father (sire), and grandparents are. Through the registration papers, a person can trace a horse's family tree back many, many years. The books (and electronic files) that record horses' bloodlines or family trees are so important that they're kept under lock and key.

If a horse's birth certificate is that important, how important do you think your birth certificate is? Have you ever seen yours? It's one of the most important documents of your life because it says what your legal name is, lists your parents, tells when you were born, and what hospital and town you were born in.

Have you ever noticed how important that information is to God? There are entire chapters in the Bible that record the fathers and mothers and children of families. Sometimes I yawn when I read the odd-looking names that are difficult to pronounce. I wonder why God included them.

Finally I figured it out. God is all about families. After all, one of the very first things He created was a family—Adam and Eve. Families are just as important to Him today as they were thousands of years ago. The most important family you can ever be part of is *His* family. Jesus talked about being "born again," and when you accept Him as your Savior, that's what happens (John 3:3-7). That's when you become a member of His family. Since Jesus is called the "King of kings," you become the King's kid! Wow!

If God provided birth certificates, what would yours look like? Why not create one?

Lord, show us how important our heavenly
"birth certificate" is. Amen.

• Just for Fun •

What is the oldest breed of horse in the world? A lot of people claim it's the Arabian, a horse that belonged to the Bedouin people, a nomadic tribe in Arabia. The Arabian adapted to the harsh weather of the desert by being able to survive on very little food and even less water. I enjoyed reading about the Bedouins and their horses on the Internet.

I like to read about animals in the Bible too. Did you know that King Solomon had 12,000 horses? He even imported some from Egypt (1 Kings 10, verses 26 and 28)!

19

The Lie

Do not steal. Do not lie.
Do not deceive one another.

Leviticus 19:11

I pulled the saddle off Dancer's back. Instantly she shifted her weight to her left side and cocked her right hind leg, and held it as if it hurt. I checked the foot. Puzzled, I shook my head. "I don't understand it, Dancer. You're gimpy again today." I grunted as I heaved the saddle onto a saddle rack in the back end of my horse trailer. I walked over to her and stroked her neck. "And all we did today was walk." I unbuckled her halter and turned her loose in the pasture. I stood with my hands on my hips, watching her saunter away. Clop, clop, clop, clump. *What could be wrong?*

I glanced at my watch. *I'd better hurry up.* I was meeting a guy named Mark to have him sign Dancer's registration papers over to me. When I'd submitted the forms to the Tennessee Walking Horse registry, they'd told me I'd used the wrong forms and I needed them signed by the previous registered owner. When I'd called the trainer I bought Dancer from, he told me he hadn't registered her, so I needed to contact the owner before him—Mark. So I did, and we set up a time to meet at his office.

I got cleaned up, jumped into my pickup, and a half hour later I was laying out the papers on Mark's desk.

As he picked up a pen, he asked, "How's that mare working out for you?"

I leaned back in the chair and nervously twisted part of my long, blond hair. "She's a good-looking horse. I bought her last year but didn't have a chance to ride her because the smoke from the forest fires was so thick. I've ridden her a couple times this year, but every time we get back home she's lame. I'm baffled."

Mark's green eyes hardened. "Didn't he tell you?"

My eyebrows puckered as I wondered what he was talking about. "Tell me what?"

He growled, "What a skunk! When I owned her, that mare broke her hind leg."

I felt the blood drain out of my face. A horse breaking a leg is very serious. I gasped, "What?"

Mark twisted the pen in his hands. His eyes squinted in anger. "When I sold her, I told the buyer all about how she'd broken her leg and I'd nursed her back to health. I told him she could never be ridden because of the damage done. He assured me that he wanted the horse as a pet for his wife." He looked me in the eyes. "I'm not lying. My neighbors were there, and they heard me tell him the whole story. I'm sure they'll write a statement supporting this if you'd like one."

I walked out of Mark's office holding the signed papers. The trainer had tricked me. My tummy felt sick. Sick that I'd unknowingly hurt Dancer by riding her. Sick that the trainer had lied to me. And sick because horses rarely recover from broken legs. Obviously Dancer hadn't recovered enough to be a saddle horse. Things kept getting worse. What next?

• Just Between You and Me •

Has anyone hurt you by telling a lie about you? Or hurt someone else by lying to you? Or maybe you've lied. After all, what is an itsy-bitsy lie? We've all heard of "white lies." But did you know there's no such thing as a harmless or little lie? Too often lies never end. They get repeated by people who aren't aware that they were lied to. And so lies grow and multiply, deeply hurting a lot of people.

Did you know that when someone tells a lie, most of the time, they end up telling another lie to cover up the first one? Before they know it, they've told so many lies that they don't know the truth. A good example is the trainer who sold me Dancer. First he lied to Mark by saying he was buying the sorrel mare as a pet. Then he sold her to me for a hefty profit. The trainer lied many times when I asked him about her health. By then the lie had grown to the size of Goliath-the-giant. The trainer must have also lied to the veterinarian so he'd get a positive health report to give to me. All those lies added up. And now I was out a saddle horse and plenty of money. And because of the lies, I'd unknowingly hurt Dancer by riding her.

Did you know that God commands us not to lie? Have you ever wondered why? It's because God is truth. A lie is the opposite of truth, so when a person speaks a lie they are ignoring God. Lying is a sin, and that sin hooks the person into agreeing with the devil, who opposes God any way possible. I don't know about you, but that's a scary thought to me. I don't want to be anywhere close to agreeing with the devil.

The good news is that our God is willing to forgive people who lie. To get a clean slate with God, all we need to do is confess what we've done, ask for His forgiveness, and then don't lie anymore. God's love will heal the wounds.

Lord, when we're tempted to speak things we know
aren't true, please remind us how serious lying is. Amen.

• Just for Fun •

What does a veterinarian do when he's hired for a pre-purchase health check on a horse? Basically, the vet gives the horse a physical exam similar to the one you get when you go the doctor. The exam can be very basic and short or long and detailed, depending on what the purchaser wants and is willing to pay for. You can find all kinds of information on the Internet about what to look for when buying a horse and why a vet check is so important.

20

X-rays

He heals the brokenhearted.

Psalm 147:3

The clinic smelled like medicine and horses. But that's not why I nervously held my breath. The veterinarian clipped the X-ray of my horse Dancer's hind leg to the light box, and then he flipped on the switch. The image glowed. With his finger, the doctor traced some shadows. He explained, "This is where the leg was broken. See how close it is to the stifle?"

I looked closely at the knee-like joint and nodded.

The doctor tapped the joint on the film and explained that the break in the bone weakened the joint so much that the horse wasn't able to support herself fully on the leg. Her body was repairing itself by fusing the two bones together into one solid bone—without the "hinge" in the middle. Eventually Dancer wouldn't be able to bend the leg at all. He ran his fingers through his hair and sighed. "Unfortunately, there isn't anything that can be done. Nobody will ever be able to ride her."

My heart pounded and my mind whirled. *I can't ever ride her? Not even at a walk? What use is a broken horse? She's worthless.* Tears streamed down my face as I loaded Dancer into the horse trailer and closed the back door. *I don't need a lawn ornament. I bought her to ride.* I pulled the truck out onto the highway and turned toward home. *Should I try to sell her?* My stomach churned. When I'd purchased her a year ago, my retired horse, Czar, had fallen in love with her. He'd never had a close horse friend until Dancer showed up. It was love at first sight for them. They'd become inseparable to the point that they shared blades of grass, sips of water out of the stock tank, and licks on the salt block. *Could I sell her? Could I do that to Czar? He'd be heart-broken.* My mind argued with itself. *But she's broken. She doesn't have any worth as a saddle horse. It would be way too expensive to keep her if I can't use her. I have to sell her.*

Gravel crunched under the tires as I pulled onto my dirt road. My horses and mule in the pasture lifted their heads and watched. Czar arched his neck, his black mane fluttering in the light breeze. His nostrils pumped in and out as he tried to smell who was in the trailer. Suddenly his bay-colored body shook and he whinnied as he raced toward me.

From within the trailer Dancer neighed an answer. The trailer rocked as she impatiently pawed to get out. The two horses acted as if they'd been apart for years instead of hours. Czar pranced along-side the fence until I pulled the pickup and trailer next to the gate and parked. I opened the back door, unloaded Dancer, and led her to the gate. The whole time Czar was chortling questions. I imagined he was saying, "Where have you been, Dancer? What took you so long? No matter. I'm so glad you're home!"

I led Dancer through the green gate and shut it, and then I unbuckled her halter. The two horses whickered and smelled each other from head to toe before wandering off so close together their sides touched.

Throughout the next week my mind was a battleground. I watched the two horses lovingly groom each other. *I can't bear the thought of separating them.* Then I'd reason, *What good is a broken horse standing in the pasture? All she'll do is eat. But who would buy a broken horse? Or what if someone bought her for cheap and turned around and sold her again as a riding horse? Then she might end up in pain the rest of her life. I can't bear that thought. God, what do I do?* Day-after-day my mind argued. *It's expensive keeping horses. There are bills for shoeing and hay.*

My mind fought until I walked past my desk and saw the last vet bill. *How many more vet bills will I have to pay for her?* I chewed on my bottom lip. *If I can't sell her, I'll have to give her away. She's not worth anything to me.*

Suddenly I heard God's booming voice in my spirit: "She's not?" I blinked in shock and took a minute to listen.

Does everything have to have a dollar value?

Yes, Dancer had a broken leg so I couldn't ride her. But she was giving me something I'd always hoped for. Ever since she'd arrived, Czar arched his neck. His youthful step returned. She'd given him a reason to live. That friendship wasn't worthless; it was priceless. Peace spread through my heart. "Okay, Lord, she's staying, but You'll have to work everything out."

• Just Between You and Me •

Have you ever felt like you were worthless? Do you worry that you're not smart enough or good-looking enough? Perhaps you don't think you have the right clothes, or makeup, or tech gadgets. Is your concern that you don't hang out with the "in" crowd? Or perhaps you have a disability of some kind...or even a broken heart.

You are not worthless! The idea that you might be worthless is a lie from the devil! He wants to push out truth and plant that negative idea in your heart. And worst of all, he tries to get you to believe that God thinks you're worthless too. But that's far from the truth.

What does God think about you? Jesus said, "What is the price of two sparrows—one copper coin? But not a single sparrow can fall to the ground without your Father knowing it. And the very hairs on your head are all numbered. So don't be afraid; *you are more valuable to God* than a whole flock of sparrows" (Matthew 10:29-31 NLT). "God loved the world so much that he gave his one and only Son, so that *everyone* who believes in him will not perish but have eternal life" (John 3:16). God loves you so much that He knows everything about you—even how many hairs are on your head. Wow! God thinks you're priceless. And I think you're amazing; after all, you love horses like I do.

Lord, show us how valuable we are to You. Amen.

• Just for Fun •

What kinds of jobs do horses do if they aren't being used as a saddle horse, a race horse, or pulling a carriage or cart?

Some horses are used for therapy—physical and emotional. Type "therapy horses" in an Internet search engine, and you'll discover the wonderful things that horses are trained to do to help people.

Another reason people keep horses is for friendship. Many horses are big love bugs. My horses even give me hugs! They put their necks over one of my shoulders and pull me next to them. Another thing they like to do is get really close and press their noses on my belly to snuggle.

Dream-horse Czar and horse-crazy Rebecca.*

21

Betrayed

*Have nothing to do with the fruitless deeds
of darkness, but rather expose them.*

Ephesians 5:11

I sat in my studio with my elbows on my desk and buried my face in my hands. I felt like a black cloud was smothering me. My mind growled, *Someone has got to stop this! This is wrong!* Even though Dancer had been examined by a veterinarian before I bought her, he hadn't known she'd broken her leg. I was heartbroken when my own veterinarian X-rayed her and said that her leg had been broken so badly that now it was fusing into one bone without a joint. She could never be used as a riding horse.

My thoughts raced like stampeding horses. I looked out the window. The rising sun was poking through the thick, black clouds that hung over the mountains. I tapped my pen on the desk. *How could someone do something this wicked? That trainer had deliberately taken a broken horse and sold her as if she was healthy. He used her to make a lot of money. How did he get Dancer to pass the health inspection? Did he drug her to numb her pain so she wouldn't limp? Did he substitute a different horse that looked like her? Either way was illegal. And he was a well-known trainer. How many times has he cheated people this way?*

I glanced at the clock. It was time to feed the horses their breakfast. I slipped into my Carhartt jacket and my muck boots and walked down to the barn. I tossed hay into the feeders and watched Dancer gimp over to the feeder with Czar. My heart ached. I figured it was too late to get my money back. Besides, if I had to give Dancer to him, who knows what he would do to her or with her. Dancer had been betrayed. She was an innocent animal that the trainer had cruelly used to carry out his scheme.

God, what can I do? What should I do? I leaned my back against the barn and watched my animals. *I have to stop that trainer from cheating someone else and hurting more animals. But how?* Over the next few days I prayed, asking God to give me a plan. And He did. It was going to take a lot of courage. I took a deep breath. I could do this.

I called Mark, the previous registered owner, and arranged to get the written statement from his neighbors who were there when he'd sold Dancer. The paper said Mark had told the trainer about the horse's broken leg before the trainer had purchased her. Next, I made an appointment with the veterinarian who had signed the pre-purchase health certificate—the paper that guaranteed the horse was healthy and sound.

When I showed up at the doctor's office, I carried a stack of papers, including the ones from my veterinarian and Mark's neighbors. After introducing myself, I shared the story and laid each sheet of paper in front of him. I said, "You see, we've been duped." The doctor's face faded white with fear. I continued. "I know you didn't do this on purpose, but it can hurt your reputation as a veterinarian." I looked him in the eyes. "I won't say anything against you, but the trainer's lying needs to stop. I need your help."

The doctor tipped his head to the side and raised his eyebrows.

"Would you please tell the other veterinarians in the valley what this trainer has done to you so that they won't be deceived by him like you and I were?"

He agreed.

I was shaking when I walked out of his office. I don't like confrontations, and it had been hard for me. But I had accomplished what I'd set out to do. I exposed the trainer for who he was. At first he might try to hire a veterinarian from out of the area who wouldn't know about his deceitful ways. But eventually the word would get out, and he'd have to stop his illegal practices. By the time I stepped into my truck, I felt as if the dark cloud that had swallowed me was gone. I knew I'd done the right thing.

• Just Between You and Me •

Were you surprised at what I did? Afterward, I was. Normally I like to forgive and forget because most of the time that is what I believe we're supposed to do as Christ followers. But God shared with me that there are times when we need to expose wickedness so that it stops. The reason I took action this way was because the trainer was breaking the law and hurting people and animals. The hard part was forgiving the trainer for what he'd done. Yes, I did that too.

When you see something that's wrong, what do you usually do?

How can you decide what to do? Should you forgive and move on? Expose and forgive? What should you do? First pray. Ask God what He'd like you to do. Next, talk with an adult you trust to get advice. Most of all, remember that God requires you to forgive.

Lord, give us the courage to do
what You know is right. Amen.

• Just for Fun •

Any horse trainer can create a fancy webpage and talk big about who he or she is. How can you find a trustworthy trainer? A great place to start is by asking the folks who live in your area and work with horses. You can also look for a trainer who has been certified by a reputable organization, such as the American Quarter Horse Association with their Professional Horsemen Association. But the first thing to do is to pray and ask God to lead you.

22

I'm Sorry

*Today I am giving you a choice. You can choose
life and success or death and disaster.*

Deuteronomy 30:15 CEV

The light summer breeze rustled the tall grass in the pasture. I took one last swipe with the currycomb on my sorrel mare's slick, summer coat. With a heavy heart I unbuckled her halter and turned her loose. I glanced up at the mountains. It was July, and the snow had melted off the tallest peaks. My heart ached with the memories of the years I'd worked from the saddle and rode horseback every day. I missed it. Even more so this year because I didn't have a healthy horse I could ride.

Dancer strolled over to Czar, and the two of them strode away. I shook my head and whined to God as I walked back to the house. *Everything has gone wrong, Lord. I bought another horse, yet I still don't have one to ride. This isn't fair! God, how did this happen?*

Inside my spirit I heard God whisper, "You didn't ask Me before you bought Dancer."

I stopped and frowned. *What?*

Over the next few minutes, God shared that I'd been busy running my own world. I never asked for *His* advice before I'd purchased Dancer. I gasped when He said that two times He'd warned me, but I'd chosen to ignore Him. When I thought back, I knew He was right. The first time was when the seller had done the pre-purchase veterinarian check without me being there. I sighed when I thought of the day the trainer had handed me the paperwork. I remembered the scratchy feeling in my spirit. It must have been the Holy Spirit trying to tell me that something was wrong. *Why hadn't I listened? Why didn't I question the trainer? Why didn't I refuse to accept the health certificate?* It all made sense now. That's why the trainer wouldn't let me be there when he did the pre-purchase health check. He had to cover up his lies. The trainer had known that my veterinarian had been the doctor who had taken the original X-rays of Dancer's broken leg, so the trainer didn't dare use him. Instead, he chose an unsuspecting doctor to deceive.

The second time God warned me was when I'd brought Dancer home, and she'd limped when I unloaded her from the trailer. Once again, I'd had an uneasy feeling, but I'd buried it under the excitement of getting a new horse.

My stomach churned as I hopped into my red-and-gray pickup and drove into town to go grocery shopping. I felt awful. I'd whined to God about the problems in my life as if I was blaming Him. But I was the one who'd created the problem. I'd chosen to live and make choices my own way.

I gripped the steering wheel. "God, I'm sorry for not asking You, and then for not listening to what You had to say. Please forgive me. Help me make sense of this mess I've created. Please let me know what to do now. Amen."

I breathed a sigh of relief and turned onto the highway. As I headed toward town, I relaxed because I knew God would help me sort everything out.

• Just Between You and Me •

Have you heard people blame God for what's gone wrong in their lives? Have you done that? On that fateful day, I was surprised to discover that I'd forgotten to ask God about buying Dancer. I was shocked that I'd ignored God! Afterward, I wondered how many times I'd done that—ignored God and then blamed Him for my troubles.

Was it right for me to blame God when He'd warned me and I didn't listen? I'm sure you know the answer to that one. If someone blames you for something that's not your fault, how do you feel? How do you think God would feel in that situation?

God loves us so much that He lets us make our own choices. That's called giving us "free will." He even lets us do things that He doesn't agree with, such as purchasing a horse without asking for or heeding His advice.

God wants us to ask His opinion beforehand. And then He wants us to follow His advice. The good news is that if we don't and find ourselves in a mess, all we need to do is be sorry, tell Him we're sorry, and ask Him what to do. God will always forgive us. And then He'll lead us out of our troubles. However, we still have to work through the consequences of our choices.

God had a wonderful solution for my situation with Dancer. I almost can't wait for you to get through the next few chapters to see what happened!

Lord, help us be quick to run to You when we've made
a mistake and say we're sorry. Amen.

• Just for Fun •

Dancer had a slick coat because of the season of the year. It was summer. In fall, the cooler weather and the lower levels of sunlight cause a horse's body to produce thicker fur coats so they can stay warm throughout the winter.

23

Fingerprints of God

[God's Spirit] knows us far better than we know ourselves...
That's why we can be so sure that every detail in our lives
of love for God is worked into something good.

Romans 8:27-28 MSG

The tires of my Dodge pickup truck hummed on the highway. My mind was consumed with the conversation I'd had with God a few moments ago. I'd made some really big blunders when I purchased Dancer because I hadn't asked God about it, and I'd ignored the Holy Spirit's prompting to be concerned. So I'd apologized to God, and then I asked Him to show me how to make sense of my mess.

Mile after mile of green fields rolled past. In one of the pastures, a gangly colt romped through the tall grass toward its mom. It tossed its head. Its curly, short mane fluttered. I giggled as the colt flattened into a dead-out run. Suddenly it locked its legs and skidded to a stop. Dirt flew. The horse kicked, bucked, and reared up to beat the air before spinning 180 degrees and taking off in the other direction.

Oh, I love watching babies play, I thought. From the cobwebs in my mind came a dream I'd had long ago of breeding a mare and getting a mule colt. I'd raised many horse colts, but not a mule colt. It would be great to have a pack animal for packing into the mountains. *I wonder if I could have Dancer bred? Would her previously broken leg be able to handle the extra weight of a pregnancy? But it's already the end of July. Is it too late in the year?* Many horses in Montana are bred in May so they give birth in April. That way the babies have a chance to grow strong and hardy before the brutal winter storms arrive.

I was lost in a dream world as the businesses that lined both sides of the highway flashed past. My veterinarian's clinic stood on the right side of the road. It almost seemed to glow. Suddenly, I heard in my spirit, "Stop and get an appointment about breeding Dancer."

"But," I argued, "my veterinarian is always booked two to three weeks in advance. That would make it way too late for Dancer this year."

God's voice seemed to boom. "Stop now!"

Instantly I remembered how I'd ignored His voice when buying Dancer. I pulled into the vet's parking lot, shut off the engine, hopped out of the truck, and trudged up the wooden steps. The receptionist greeted me by name. I told her I'd like an appointment to breed a horse.

The receptionist flipped through the appointment book. "How about tomorrow?"

My heart skipped a beat. *Tomorrow? The doctor never has openings! Could this be a God thing?* I grinned and boldly asked, "How about today?"

She glanced at the schedule and then at her watch. "It's eleven o'clock now. Could you have her here by one?"

Nodding I said, "Write in my name. We'll be here."

• Just Between You and Me •

Have you asked God to help you out of a mess and then watched with surprise as He worked a miracle? Something that was so big and awesome that you had to pinch yourself to believe it was real? That's what God did for me that day. And He did it because He loves me. And I know He loves you too, so He'll do the same for you.

Lord, help us believe absolutely that You
want the best for us. Amen.

· Just for Fun ·

Did you know that different kinds of animals have different "gestational" periods—the length of time the females are pregnant before delivering their babies? "Gestation" is how long it usually takes for a baby to be fully formed inside of its mom's womb and be ready to be born. Here are some general gestation or pregnancy times:

- hamsters, 16 to 23 days
- dogs, 63 days
- cats, 62 to 64 days
- horses, 320 to 362 days (an average of 11 months and two days)
- elephants, 2 years!
- humans, 280 days (9 months)

24

God's Clock

Timing is the Father's business.

Acts 1:7 MSG

The smell of medicine hung in the cool air at the vet clinic. My sorrel mare was tied to a metal chute. The doctor examined her previously injured leg. Earlier God had prodded me to bring her in today to determine if she could physically handle being pregnant with her leg being in such bad shape. Several times the doctor picked up the leg and tried to bend it at the joint. The bones had already started to fuse into one, forming what I call a "peg leg." (I picture a pirate with a wooden leg.) Dancer's leg joint didn't flex much at all. He untied her and had me walk her while he watched how she carried herself.

After that he clicked on the light box and clipped up Dancer's leg X-ray. After examining it, he turned the light off and turned to me. Peering over the top of his glasses, he said, "I don't see any reason why you can't breed her. Her leg is fusing together, so it'll be strong enough to support her and a baby. There's only one thing left to check. Would you like me to ultrasound her womb to see if it looks healthy and to see when she could be bred?"

My heart raced as my mind took in what he was asking. Now that I knew that Dancer's leg could physically handle it, was I ready to go to the next step? Did I want to have her bred this year? In my spirit I asked God, "What do *You* think?" Peace washed over me. Everything was flowing together so smoothly. I felt like I was living by God's clock, by God's timing. I nodded.

The metal stand that held the ultrasound equipment rumbled as the doctor rolled it across the concrete floor and positioned it next to Dancer. He smeared the red hair on her abdomen with jelly-like goo, which would help carry the sound waves. After he flipped on the switches, a screen lit up. He rubbed the wand over her flank. The image of her guts flashed on the screen. In fascination, I leaned forward as the doctor gave me a "tour." Suddenly he chuckled. "Do you have a father picked out for the baby?"

I looked at him blankly.

He shook his head, "This is unbelievable. Some people try to do this for years and aren't able to. Why, it's perfect timing. She'll be ready to be bred in two days." He took off his glasses and once again asked, "Do you have a father picked out?"

I stood there and stammered. "I...I...looked at one a few years ago, but I don't know if he's still available."

"This might be the last chance to breed her this year. If we're going to get this done, we'll have to act fast. You're welcome to use my phone—call now."

Over the next few minutes I was shocked to learn that the father was available—but only for the next couple of days because the owner was going out of town. We agreed on a breeding price and made the arrangements. Once again everything was going according to God's clock. I was running on God's standard time.

• Just Between You and Me •

Have you experienced a time when everything seemed to fall into place? When God asked you to do something and you did it, and then miracle after miracle unfolded to make everything work? Did it almost feel like God had planned the situation a long time ago?

When this happens to me, I'm reminded of the Bible verse that talks about when God created mankind: "He marked out their appointed times in history and the boundaries of their lands" (Acts

17:26). When you get into this groove, it feels natural because God knows the future. He planned it. He even planned when you were going to be born! Have you ever thought about that? Nobody or no thing is a mistake in God's timing.

When you were born, God didn't say, "Wow, where did she come from?" Even if you were a surprise to your parents, you were planned by God. And God loves you so much that He made great plans for your life!

Lord, please lead us into the great plans
You have for us. Amen.

• Just for Fun •

Have you watched an ultrasound being done? The machine sends sound waves into the body. They "bounce off" internal objects and are reflected back. The machine interprets those waves and creates an image on the monitor. The images look like photographs. They can be difficult to read if you're not used to it. The whole process is fascinating and an important tool to figure out health problems in humans and horses.

To see an ultrasound image, type in "ultrasound images of a baby" on the Internet.

25

The Challenge

Grow a wise heart—you'll do yourself a favor.

Proverbs 19:8 MSG

I stroked the white blaze on Dancer's forehead. The doctor's voice echoed off the concrete walls of the examining room in the veterinary clinic. "I can't promise this will work." He explained that it was tricky to breed a mare to get a mule colt. A mule is a "hybrid" animal. That means two species are bred to get a mule. I took mental notes as the vet laid out the challenges.

"If the mare gets upset or gets nervous, her body might 'slough the colt.'"

My eyebrows drew together. I'd heard that before. If for some reason the mare doesn't want to be pregnant, she'll abort her own baby. Dancer was a nervous mare already. *How am I going to keep her calm?* I wondered. *She doesn't even like coming to the clinic. God, how do I do this so that she'll carry the baby full-term so it will be born healthy?*

The doctor gave me some pointers. "Don't change anything. Keep her routine the same. When you bring her on Saturday, it would be wise to bring your own hay so she's getting what she's used to. Be sure to write down the feeding schedule for us."

I nodded and thought about her routine. Her whole day centered around Czar. She was head-over-heels in love with my old saddle horse. A crazy thought popped into my mind. *Maybe I should bring him in too? He doesn't get upset about anything, and she'd be happy and calm as long as he was here.* I waited until the doctor paused and then hesitantly explained my thought. "Her best friend is my old gelding. Would it be okay if I brought him in to keep her calm?"

The doctor grinned at my request. "If we've got a stall for him, that'd be fine." Over the next few minutes he finished briefing me, and we lined out a plan for the breeding to occur.

I untied Dancer and led her outside. Her hooves crunched on the gravel driveway behind me. I was nearly skipping with joy. My dream was coming true! If everything went right, Dancer would be pregnant in a couple days. I loaded her into the trailer, latched the doors shut, and said a brief prayer: "God, please keep Dancer calm, and give me the wisdom to know exactly what to do to make this dream come true. Amen."

• Just Between You and Me •

Have you faced a monster problem or huge challenge? How did you find the solution? For years I stumbled through life as I tried to figure out what to do. I finally realized that no matter how many years I lived, I couldn't figure out everything by myself. I needed more wisdom.

When I hear the word "wisdom," it sounds old, and I picture an old man with a long, white beard sitting on a porch in a rocking chair. And in a way that's true. Wisdom takes time to discover and learn. I chuckle when I hear people say that wisdom means "learning from other people's mistakes, so you don't have to make the same ones." How would you like to be able to solve your monster problems without making so many mistakes? I sure would.

What I've learned is that I can ask God to lead me to people who have more experience about the situation than I do. For instance, with Dancer, that person was my vet. I then pepper the person with questions and carefully listen to the advice he or she offers. Then I check with God to see what He thinks and what He'd like me to do.

What does that mean for you and me? We don't have to be old to be wise or act on wisdom. We only have to check with God, ask the right people for advice, check with God again, and then move forward. Do you think this process will work for you when you face your next problem?

Lord, teach us how to be wise beyond our years. Amen.

• Just for Fun •

Did you know that mules are a hybrid animal? They are the offspring from two different species of animals. Mules have a horse mom and a donkey dad. The offspring of a horse dad and donkey mom is called a hinny.

Because many hybrid animals are infertile, meaning they can't create babies, mules usually can't be bred to each other. That's why people have to breed a horse with a donkey.

26

Favor of God

*My God will meet all your needs according
to the riches of his glory in Christ Jesus.*

Philippians 4:19

The sun was barely awake on Saturday morning when I nervously leaned my elbows on the tall front counter at the veterinarian clinic. I rubbed my forehead. "But, God," I silently prayed, "what went wrong?" I looked up slowly and said, "But I need a stall where I can put Czar and Dancer together."

The lady behind the desk peered over her reading glasses. "The only corrals large enough for two are reserved for stallions." Her nostrils pinched as she added, "And they're all full."

I sighed. "Okay, I admit I'm a mother hen. Dancer is a nervous mare. She's going to be here for two days, and Dancer and Czar need to be together. Will you please check to be sure?"

The receptionist shrugged her shoulders. I think I saw her roll her eyes as she disappeared into the back room.

The veterinarian told me it was important to keep Dancer's daily routine the same. The most important thing was to make sure that she didn't get upset or nervous while she stayed at the clinic to be bred. Because she and Czar spent every waking moment together, I knew that I had to bring him too. Without him, Dancer would be an emotional mess.

A couple days ago when I reserved the stall for Dancer, I was told there wouldn't be enough room for both of them in one stall...unless it was a stall reserved for studs, but they were all full. The office people had pleasantly said they could reserve two stalls, but they couldn't promise they'd be next to each other. I knew that wouldn't work. Czar and Dancer had to be in the same stall. I immediately pleaded with God: *Please heal up one of the stallions, and send him home so Dancer and Czar can be together when I bring them in.*

I heard soft footsteps whispering down the hall toward me. The receptionist's face looked stiff as she walked over to her desk and rifled through her appointment book. Glancing up, she matter-of-factly said, "One of the stallions was released early. He went home last night. They're cleaning his stall now. It'll be ready in ten minutes."

In my mind I screamed, *Yes! God, You did it! Wahoo!*

• Just Between You and Me •

Have you ever had something like this happen for you? When it was obvious that God had worked everything out behind the scenes? When it happens for me, I call it the "favor of God" because I feel like a favorite child being taken care of by my doting Father in heaven.

Can you relate? How do you feel when it happens for you? Do you remember to thank Him?

Lord, thank You for showing us that You care about us and will provide for our every need. Amen.

• Just for Fun •

Why are stallions kept in a separate corral at a veterinarian's clinic? Most stallions have an aggressive nature. Some don't like other male horses because they're competition for the mares, so stallions will bite and kick them. To keep the peace, the stalls for stallions are usually separated by distance or by solid walls.

27

The Secret Weapon

I run toward the goal, so that I can win
the prize of being called to heaven.

Philippians 3:14 CEV

I unlocked the rear door on my white horse trailer. It groaned as it swung open. It felt like a million butterflies were fluttering in my tummy. Today I was dropping Czar and Dancer by the veterinarian clinic to have Dancer bred. The doctor said that I had to keep Dancer from getting upset. The problem was, she was a Nervous Nelly, so I'd asked God to show me exactly what to do. I stepped into the trailer and wondered, *Did I remember everything?* Czar's head swung around as I opened his stall door. I stepped next to him and ruffled his black mane. I coached him. "It's your job is to keep Dancer happy, okay?"

He merely nodded his head, as if to say, "Quit dawdling. Let's get on with the show." Chuckling, I brought him out and tied him to the side of the trailer. After unloading Dancer, I led the two of them side-by-side to the large corral (the one God had reserved for them) and turned them loose. They sniffed the wood shavings that covered the ground, trying to smell the horses that had been there before them. Dancer paced along the fence, back and forth, even though Czar was there with her. I calmly said, "Dancer, you can settle down now. Everything's going to be fine."

Quickly I unloaded the bales of hay and stacked them outside the corral gate. Next to the hay I set a bucket of grain and some grain pans. Even though I tossed a flake of hay in the feeder, Dancer still nervously paced. I took a deep breath. *It's time for the secret weapon.* Just before I'd driven out my driveway, God had reminded me to bring the one thing that I'd used in the past to set an atmosphere of peace for Dancer. I reached in the tack compartment of the trailer and pulled out the boom box and a package of batteries.

After loading the batteries into the compartment, I set the boom box on the stack of hay and turned it on. *This better work!* A fuzzy hissing noise broke the silence. I grabbed the antennae and extended it to full height. After drawing it in a circle, the signal came in clearly and the melodious notes of K-LOVE radio drifted through the barnyard. Instantly Dancer stopped pacing. She stared at the radio. Gradually, her muscles rippled as they relaxed and she lowered her head.

I sat on the pile of hay and swung my legs. I wanted to make sure that Dancer settled in before I left. When I turned to leave, I noticed the doctor standing with his clipboard, staring in wonder at the radio. The hay prickled me as I uncomfortably shifted my weight. *How long has he been standing there?* I glanced at the doctor's puzzled face and then sideways at the radio. *It doesn't look like he's had anybody else bring a radio before.* He peered over his spectacles at me. I felt my face flush bright red and I stammered, "You said...to keep her calm...She likes K-LOVE radio."

The doctor's eyebrows drew together. He paused a few minutes as he slowly glanced at the pile of hay...grain...and grain pans. "Glad you're settling in." Then he turned to leave.

I watched him walk away. *I guess I remembered everything. Maybe I have gone a little overboard, but as long as it works, who cares?*

• Just Between You and Me •

Have you gone overboard when you've done something? "Going overboard" means doing more than most people would in a similar circumstance. If you have, you're in good company. In order to win a race, a competition, or to become a professional, people usually have to go overboard. Champions go the extra distance and accomplish extraordinary things. They put their whole hearts into winning by setting goals and practicing consistently.

Did you know that the same is true in our spiritual lives? If we want to be champions for Jesus, if we want to become more like Him, it's important to set goals. Have you considered setting goals, such as reading one chapter in the Bible and praying every day? If you haven't, why not start now?

Lord, give us the passion to be champions for You. Amen.

• Just for Fun •

Have you watched the horse jumping competition in the Olympics? How old do you think the youngest person who competed was?

A person has to be 18 years old to compete. In 2012, the world watched in awe as 18-year-old Reed Kessler rode as a competitor—the youngest person to ever do that. To find out more, check her out on the Internet.

28

Horse Crazy

If you will obey my voice indeed, and keep my covenant, then you shall be a peculiar treasure to me above all people.

Exodus 19:5 KJV

The morning sun's rays shone from behind the tall mountains, crowning them with golden spokes. The diesel engine in my red-and-gray Dodge rattled as I drove next to Czar and Dancer's corral at the veterinarian clinic and parked. Yesterday Dancer had been bred, and although it was early morning, I had an appointment with the doctor. He was going to ultrasound Dancer to see if she "took." I leaned forward and stared at my red mare. *Is she pregnant?* I jumped out of the truck. Both horses nickered a hello. My heart thumped wildly. I'd always been horse crazy—embarrassingly so. Although I tried to control myself when other people were around.

I opened the metal corral gate. Czar pushed his muscular bay body between me and Dancer—almost as if blocking me. I scratched the white star on his face. "Are you jealous?"

I sidestepped to the left. Czar's body puffed up at attention. He moved forward and cut me off. I frowned. *What's he doing? I've owned him more than 25 years, and he's never stepped in front of me like this. What's he trying to tell me?*

Moving to the right, I tried to step around Czar, but he refused to let me pass. A moment of silence passed. "Ahhh," I finally said, "are you protecting Dancer?" While nodding my head, a strange thought ran through my mind. *Does he know she's pregnant?* Instantly Czar's body relaxed, and he nuzzled me. Gently I stroked his neck and then slipped past him. *Does he think I understand? Is that why he suddenly let his guard down so I could get by him?*

I reached out to pet Dancer's neck and touch her reddish-gold mane. She refused to let me touch her. With her nose she blocked my hand. *How strange. She always loves it when I stroke her mane.* I stood frozen in place with my hand extended. Dancer rested her lips on the back of my hand, and she shallowly panted. My mind searched for answers. *What's going on? Is she trying to tell me that she's going to have a baby?*

For almost five minutes we stood transfixed, Dancer's warm breath whispered across my wrist. My arm got tired so I finally lowered it. I looked into her deep-brown eyes, "So, Dancer, are you trying to tell me you're pregnant?"

From behind me I heard, "Ahem."

I spun around.

The veterinarian stood at the gate. He peered over his spectacles at me. "Are you ready to bring her inside?"

Without thinking, I blurted, "Oh, you won't need to check her. She's pregnant. She just told me." Instantly, I turned as red as a beet.

He raised his eyebrows and almost said something, but at the last moment he looked as if he swallowed his tongue. He told me since I was there and he was there, he might as well check her over.

I agreed, so I took Dancer into the clinic.

After the doctor finished the exam, he agreed. Dancer was pregnant, and if her body chose to carry the baby, she'd deliver in 11 months or so.

I took Dancer outside, and loaded her and then Czar into the trailer. Mixed emotions whirled through my mind as I drove down the highway headed home. I was excited about the baby, but then I'd mentally kick myself for acting so foolish around the vet. *I bet the doctor is ready to commit me to the loony ward!*

I arrived home and unloaded the horses. No sooner had I gotten into the house when the phone rang. It was one of my dear friends. I told her about my embarrassing blurt at the vet's. I added, "I'm just so...so peculiar."

Jeanne laughed. "Do you know what peculiar means?"

"No."

"It means 'to be set apart for a purpose.' Your ability to communicate so well with horses is a gift from God. Don't try to hide it or apologize for it."

After I hung up, I determined that I wouldn't be embarrassed again for being horse crazy. That was a gift too. And somehow I was going to use it to tell people about God.

• Just Between You and Me •

Did you know that God has given you special gifts and talents. Oftentimes they are the very things that you get excited about. I credit God for making me horse crazy at a very early age. What has God tucked inside your heart? What do you really enjoy doing? Is there some way you can use that gift to tell people about God?

Lord, help us be thrilled with the special gifts
You've tucked inside us.
We want to use them for Your glory. Amen.

• Just for Fun •

How did Czar know Dancer was pregnant? How did Dancer know she was pregnant so soon? What happened inside Dancer's body that both animals immediately knew? The only way I can explain it is by calling it a "holy moment"—the exact time when God created a new being. Whether it's a horse or a human, life is a gift from God.

The moment when a mare becomes pregnant, a new life—totally separate from hers—immediately begins to grow inside her. The same thing happened when your mother became pregnant with you. Instantly your mom's chemical makeup in her body changed as it prepared to nurture you and give you everything you needed.

29

The Experiment

*[The Lord said,] "Before I formed you
in the womb I knew you."*

Jeremiah 1:5

My hands trembled with excitement as I read the sheets of paper I'd printed from a website. It was the timeline that listed the development of a foal while in its mother's womb. It even had photos of what the baby looked like each month. It was exactly what I was looking for so I could do my experiment. I felt like I'd found a gold mine.

My interest in interacting with a foal during pregnancy had started years ago when I'd heard about games some human mothers played with their yet-to-be-born babies. When the baby kicked, the mother would tap her fingers on the spot where the baby kicked. Soon the game would reverse. The mother would tap and the baby would kick where her fingers tapped. I'd even read stories of how babies could hear sounds outside the mother's body. Then, when they were born, they'd recognize the voices of the people who had been around their mothers—and even the music she'd played.

My mind swirled with questions. If I do these types of things with a foal, will they work the same way? Will the baby learn to recognize my voice? How will I know? Will it move in the womb and play games with me? Maybe the foal and I can get acquainted before it's born. Will it know who I am after it's born?

I took a deep breath. *God, I'm not sure where to start. What do I do?* God's still small voice spoke to my spirit: "It's easy. Just talk into the mare's belly a couple times a day. You can even sing her songs."

I set the stack of papers on the kitchen counter, raced to the back door, and pulled on my boots. I couldn't wait to say hi.

• Just Between You and Me •

Did you know that when you were still inside your mother's womb you could hear her voice? And the music she played or listened to? Isn't that awesome? I was shocked when I found out that people and their babies could be in touch with each other before they were born. For some reason, I thought unborn babies were more like blobs...growing in an isolated environment. Boy, was I wrong. Science has proven that although you can't see the baby, its tiny brain functions, and it can experience some of life through its mother's world.

Even more amazing, have you considered that God created you in your mother's womb? And that He knew you the entire time you were safely tucked away inside your mom?

God, remind us how every unborn baby is
one of Your marvelous creations. Amen.

• Just for Fun •

Although I haven't heard of anybody talking to a pregnant mare's belly, I have heard of hunting dog breeders who claim they're able to "program" puppies before they're born so they'll become better hunting dogs. Maybe someday you can do a study on unborn babies to see what they can learn while in their mothers' wombs.

30

Wind Dancer

The Lord chose me and gave me
a name before I was born.

Isaiah 49:1 CEV

I pressed the side of my face against Dancer's flank. In a singsong voice I said, "Hi, baby! Just think, you're already three days old!" I inhaled deeply, taking in the rich, sweaty, dusty smell horses have. I continued to lean my face into my mare's warm side. "So, are you a boy or a girl?" I knew God had decided that detail the instant He formed the baby. I wanted to know so I peppered God for information. *God, calling her baby seems so cold. I'd like to name her, but I don't know if she's a boy or girl. Will you help me out?*

Dancer cocked her hind leg as she relaxed. Her eyelids drooped, and she napped in the warmth of the morning sun. For the next half hour I chatted to the baby. It was strange, but the longer I stood there the more I felt God was telling my spirit that Dancer's baby was a girl. *Maybe I should give the baby a girl's name right now, even though it's not born. What would be a good name?* I stood up as I thought about it, but my mind was blank.

When I turned to leave, a light breeze stirred some aspen leaves. Suddenly a gust of wind picked them up, and the round-shaped leaves skittered. They seemed to tumble with joy, doing cartwheels and dancing across the pasture. *Look! They're dancing on the wind. Dancing...not quite it. Dancer. Oh, that's her mom's name. Wind...Dancer. Wind Dancer!* "That's it! Wind Dancer!" I said joyfully. "That's perfect! The baby will be named after her mom and the wind."

• Just Between You and Me •

Whether it's a horse or a human being, science has proven that at conception a new individual is created that is totally separate from its mother and father. It's a special combination of the DNA from both parents. The DNA determines if it's a boy or a girl, the color of its hair and eyes, and all the other physical traits.

Do you look more like your mom or your dad? Perhaps you can see a little of both of them in you. That's because your DNA is a mixture of both. You're a one-of-a-kind original made by God Himself through your parents.

Lord, thank You for making each of us one of a kind. Amen.

• Just for Fun •

DNA profiling, which is also called "DNA fingerprinting," has become widely used in horse circles. A person can take a hair from a horse's mane or tail and send it to a special laboratory that will run tests on it. The results are used to identify the horse for registration purposes and to determine its parents. It can also be used to identify stolen horses.

31

Eat Your Vitamins

*[Your GOD is] giving you a teacher to train you
how to live right—teaching, like rain out of heaven,
showers of words to refresh and nourish your soul.*

Joel 2:23 MSG

The lid rattled as I pulled it off the metal trash can where I stored the grain in the tack room. Dancer, tied up inside the barn, nickered at the sound. I was lost in my own thoughts and didn't pay attention to her. I carefully measured her special food while trying to figure out what I could do. A friend of mine was struggling, and I was wondering how best to help. I'd tried to build him up with kind words, but I felt like I hadn't said the right ones.

Dancer pawed the ground and chortled louder, as if saying, "Hello, Rebecca! I'm waiting. Where are you?"

I yelled through the open wooden door, "Be patient! I'm measuring your vitamins and minerals so your baby will grow up strong and healthy." Under my breath I whispered, "I wish there was a special formula that would make Scott powerful like a superhero." In my spirit, I heard God's voice: "You can give him the vitamins and minerals that are packed in My Word. They will build his strength from the inside out."

I nodded my head and thought about that as I stirred Dancer's mixture with a wooden spoon. There had been times in the past when I'd felt blue. My friends had shared Bible verses with me. And when I read them over and over, the words cheered me up. The words—God's truth—carried His strength into me. *Why hadn't I done that with Scott?* Although I'd talked with him about God, I hadn't given him any particular Bible verses to think about or meditate on.

Impatiently, Dancer whinnied like the burst of a trumpet. I took one last stir with the wooden spoon and stepped into the main part of the barn with the brimming pan of grain.

Dancer bobbed her head as I set the pan in front of her.

"There you go, girl. Now eat your vitamins."

Instantly she buried her nose into the feed and chewed. I stood at her side, stroking her neck. "You're sharing your vitamins with your baby, Wind Dancer. And in a few minutes I'm going to go share some spiritual ones with Scott."

• Just Between You and Me •

Did you know that "the word of God is alive and powerful" (Hebrews 4:12 NLT)? How can His Word be alive when they're just words printed on paper? It's because the words aren't just anybody's. They were given by God. That's why they have the power to strengthen and encourage us from the inside out.

When you have a hard time in school, with friends, or at home, have you gone to your room, pulled out your Bible, and asked God to show you a verse to encourage you? Have you ever shared a Bible verse with a friend as an encouragement? Why not try it next time so you can enjoy the spiritual vitamins God packed into His Word?

Please remind us, Lord, that Your Word contains the most important wisdom to share with our friends. Amen.

• Just for Fun •

When horses are pregnant, they need extra vitamins and miner-als. Making a baby is a big job, and it requires healthy, balanced food or nutrition. Good hay and a mineral block are a great place to start. In some areas you may need to add extra supplements to the food. In western Montana we have to add a mineral called selenium. So how do you find out what minerals your mare needs? Ask your veterinarian. He or she will be more than happy to coach you.

32

Miracle of the Heart

Create in me a clean heart, O God.

Psalm 51:10 NLT

I sat at my desk in the kitchen and glanced at the calendar hanging on the wall. I'd numbered each day so I could follow the development of the foal inside Dancer. It was her twenty-fourth day of being pregnant. By today, Wind Dancer's heart had grown to the size of a pea, and it was beating. She had a head with small eyes, and her tail had already started to form. *With the baby developing that much, surely Dancer will look different*, I thought. I grabbed my jacket and raced out the door.

I half-skidded down the steep, damp trail. As soon as my horses saw me, they whinnied. My mule, Little Girl, lifted her head and brayed, a long drawn-out "heeeee haaaaaaaw," which announced to the whole neighborhood, "You're finally here! It's breakfast time." I giggled, unclipped the gate latch at the bottom of the hill, and stepped into the pasture.

Soon the herd was mugging me and begging for scratches. Dancer shook her head at all of them to shoo them away. She wanted all the attention. I rubbed her shoulder. *You don't look any different today than you did a month ago.* I looked her over from head to tail. Even though she was pregnant, I couldn't tell if she'd gained any weight. I was disappointed. I wanted her to glow or something. "And you don't really act much different either—you're still your bossy self. If anyone were to walk into the pasture, they'd never guess that you're pregnant. How could they know there was another little heart beating inside of you?"

I stroked her reddish-gold mane. She closed her eyes as she relaxed. A strange thought wiggled into my mind. *There's no way to know by looking at the outside that there's a miracle growing on the inside.*

• Just Between You and Me •

By looking on the outside it's impossible to know exactly what's going on inside. Isn't that true regarding our life with Jesus? I remember when I gave my life to Christ. I looked exactly the same as I did a couple minutes before. Nobody would have known by looking at me that a miracle had happened inside, that Jesus had come into my heart and made it clean.

The only One who can look inside of you and really know what's going on is God. He sees inside your heart. And better yet, He's always had His loving eyes on you. Does that sound funny? But it's true. God sees everything. When your mother was pregnant with you and nobody could tell, God formed you inside your mother's womb. You're so important to God that no matter where you are, you're never invisible to Him.

Lord, show us today how important we are to You.
Thank You for loving us. Amen.

• Just for Fun •

Close your eyes and picture a little heart the size of a pea. Isn't it hard to imagine that such a small heart could be beating... thump...thump...thump?

When you were in your mother's womb, do you know what day your heart probably started beating? When you were around three weeks old (or approximately 22 days).

33

Old Friends

Do not forsake your friend or a friend of your family.

Proverbs 27:10

The golden aspen leaves waved in the September breeze as cool air rolled down the mountains for the evening. I strolled into the pasture for my end-of-the-day good night to Wind Dancer. For the last 61 days I'd rested my cheek against Dancer's side and chattered to her baby. Morning and night it was the same, and I always finished off by singing a little ditty or song. Thoughts of the baby swirled through my mind all day.

I walked toward Dancer in a daze. In my mind I was reviewing the baby chart I'd memorized from reading it so much. The baby now had four legs with teeny hooves. She had eyelids, and her ears were developing. Although she'd grown to the size of a hamster, she was still bald—no hair yet.

I was about to put my cheek against Dancer's side when my little red mare turned and walked away from me. My eyebrows arched as I stared at her. She'd never done that before. All the times I'd talked to her belly I hadn't used a halter because Dancer never moved. "Dancer, what are you doing? You're supposed to stand still." Dancer didn't even pause. She ambled toward the other side of the pasture.

I skipped next to her side. "Dancer, stop!" Her gaze was fixed straight ahead as she continued to chug along.

I grabbed a clump of mane and held on. "Stop! I just want to talk to your belly." Instead of stopping, she sped up. I let go of her mane and watched her trot away. She halted at the fence and wouldn't look back. I shook my head. *God, what is that about? Why would she ignore me?*

Inside my spirit I heard, "Ignore you? You've been ignoring her." Instantly my heart ached. I had ignored her the whole two months. I'd been so excited about the baby that I'd spent every spare moment with my cheek against Dancer's flank. I hadn't even groomed Dancer. Other than feeding her, I hadn't spent any quality time with her at all. *Does she feel like I've abandoned her?* If so, she was right. It was time to change that.

I dropped my eyes to the ground and slowly walked toward Dancer. I cooed, "I'm so sorry. I didn't mean to forget you." She stared straight ahead, but her red ears swiveled toward me as she listened. When I was ten feet away, I stopped. She turned her head. Holding it sideways a bit, she tipped it down as if she was peering over a pair of reading glasses, checking out everything I was saying.

I stood perfectly still. "Dancer, you're important to me too. After all, you were my friend first."

Dancer sighed. I felt like she understood. She lowered her head, walked toward me, and stopped right in front of me. With my index finger I gently traced the white blaze on her forehead. "I won't forget you again. I promise."

• Just Between You and Me •

Have you been so excited about a new friend that you accidentally ignored your other friends? What happened? How did your friends feel?

I've done that before—and not just with horses. I got so excited about getting to know the new person that my other friends faded into the background.

How can we avoid doing that? Perhaps when we meet a special new friend, we can introduce them to our other friends and go to a movie or do something together as a group.

When I figured this out, I noticed there were other times I'd gotten swept away in new adventures. All day long I thought about the exciting things coming up—so much that I brushed another friend to the side—Jesus. Have you done that too? The solution is to invite Him to be a part of our adventures. I don't want Jesus to ever feel left out of my life. How about you?

Lord, help us stay tuned in with You.
You are our best friend. Amen.

• Just for Fun •

When the foal is being formed inside of its mother, what position do you think it's in? Is it lying on its side? Lying with its feet tucked under it? The baby is lying on its back with its feet pointed up!

Since a foal has legs and hooves by the time it's 61 days old, how old do you think you were when your legs and hands began to develop? You were just 35 days old—that's just over one month. Wow!

34

So Discouraged...

*We are certain that God will hear our prayers
when we ask for what pleases him.*

1 John 5:14 CEV

The thick October clouds had suffocated the blue sky for days, casting gloomy shadows that matched the doubts in my mind. Cold rain dripped off my slicker and ran down my jeans. I set a pan of grain in front of Dancer, stepped back, and watched her chow down. Curling my cold fingers into circles, I blew my warm breath through them. *Is Dancer really pregnant?*

Every day for the last three months I'd talked into Dancer's belly and sang a little ditty to Wind Dancer. At first it was easy to believe and be excited. But day-after-day when I didn't see any changes in the mare, doubt seeped in. The last couple weeks when the clouds rolled in, my hopes and dreams felt rained on. I was wondering if God was hearing my prayers. Next week I was supposed to schedule an ultrasound to confirm if Dancer was with foal...or if she wasn't. Until then there wouldn't be any scientific proof.

I cocked my head and stared at my sorrel mare. I was so discouraged that I didn't even feel like talking to Wind Dancer. Cold questions drizzled into my mind. *How do I know she really is pregnant? She doesn't look any bigger. The vet warned me that oftentimes horses will choose to miscarry their colts. What if that happened when she was in the field and I hadn't noticed?*

I stroked Dancer's wet mane. *God, I'm weary of waiting and watching. Dancer's not even any bigger. Did You listen to my prayers? Did You really answer me or was it my imagination fueled by hope?* For a few moments I stood and listened to Dancer grinding the grain between her molars. The sound calmed me, and peace settled over me.

I sighed. *Well, I'm standing here. I might as well talk to Dancer's belly.* I rested my cheek against her wet flank. My voice wavered as I sang the daily song. Gathering all the cheer I could, I chanted with a sing-song voice, "Hi, Wind Dancer. It's wet and icky out here. What's it like in there?" A silly picture drifted through my mind—of her floating inside her mother's womb. I grinned. "I guess it's wet and icky in there too."

Suddenly, as fast as lightning, KABAM! Wind Dancer kicked in the exact spot on her mom's flank where I'd been talking. I squealed with delight! There was a baby! My prayers had been answered. All those months of waiting and believing—and the baby was for real the entire time! I didn't need to get an ultrasound for Dancer. God showed me that He was listening too, and He was answering my prayers.

• Just Between You and Me •

Have you ever prayed, and prayed, and prayed...wondering if God was doing something about your problem? Or if He even heard your prayers? Or if He even cared enough to listen to what you had to say? I have. And this was one of those days. Normally when I pray, I feel like God's standing with me. Oftentimes I receive His answers to my prayers right away. But when I have to wait for an answer, it can get harder and harder to believe that He's heard me.

Do you ever struggle like that? If you do, the best way to find hope and encouragement is to talk to God and read the Bible. In my situation with Dancer, I checked to see if what I'd prayed was what God wanted. How did I do that? I reviewed all the things He'd been impressing on my spirit over the last several months. I purposely recalled the things He'd told me and shown me through His Word to make sure I'd been following His leading. Then I asked God to send me some encouragement—and He did.

The next time you're wondering if God heard you, perhaps you could do those same two things. I bet God will give you the answer!

God, thank You for loving us so much that You listen and respond to our prayers. Amen.

• Just for Fun •

When Wind Dancer kicked me, she was a bit bigger than a chipmunk. How big were you when you were 91 days old and still in your mom's womb? You were already the size of a peach. All your vital organs—heart, liver, and so forth— were formed. Your vocal chords and teeth were developing. You were probably sucking your thumb, and you had fingernails!

35

The Best Gift

The sweet smell of incense can make you feel good,
but true friendship is better still.

Proverbs 27:9 CEV

Wispy white clouds spiraled through the winter-blue sky. The sun glittered off the snowflakes, making the pasture look like a sea of diamonds. Bundled in boots, mittens, and a hat, I nearly skipped to the barn. It was Christmas Day! My horses and mule greeted me with their usual chorus of whinnies and brays. I laughed out loud. "Merry Christmas to you too! And today you each get an extra ration of grain as a present." My friends all nodded and chortled.

While I busily loaded the sled with hay and grain, my thoughts wandered. *If I could ask for anything for Christmas, what would it be?* I pulled the sled out of the barn and into the pasture. As I tossed hay and dumped the grain into the feeders, memories of Christmases past drifted through my mind. My dad and mom made each celebration special by decorating the house, buying a fresh pine tree to decorate, and loading presents underneath. Out of all of those years, the present I remembered most was when they gave me my very own horse. It was a gift that meant so much because that horse became my best friend. It wasn't an "object" that mattered. No, it was the *relationship* that was formed between Andy and me.

I pulled the empty sled toward the barn. When I passed Dancer, she waggled her head and flipped up her lip to say "thank you."

I giggled at her silly face. If someone gave me all the money in the world, I couldn't buy what is important to me—my relationships with God, friends, and my critters. I already have the best gifts there are!

• Just Between You and Me •

Have you noticed that after a few months have passed since you received special gifts, like for your birthday or Christmas, it's hard to remember what you received? Maybe you asked for and got some special games, but after playing with them a bazillion times they weren't so important anymore. Why do you think that is?

I believe it's because the most important things in life aren't objects. I'm sure that the best gifts are the *relationships* we have with Jesus, our family members, and our friends. Instead of growing old and getting tired of them, the longer we have close relationships the more valuable they become.

And one way we show people we care about them is giving gifts. It's fun exchanging presents with friends, isn't it? But did you know that *you* can be a gift to your family and friends? Perhaps you can help your friends with their homework or go to a concert or play they're involved in. Maybe you can pick up your room without being asked or do something nice for your mom, or dad, or brother, or sister. What other things could you do to show people how special they are to you? How can you be a gift to Jesus?

Show us, Lord, how to be the best gifts we can be
to You, to our families, and to our friends. Amen.

• Just for Fun •

Do people feed horses differently in the winter than they do in the summer? In the northern states where we get snow and cold weather, the horses will be able to stay warmer if they're fed more grain and hay in the winter. I like to watch the weather report and feed them extra rations several hours before a storm hits. That way the food has been digested, and they have ready energy to fight off the cold.

Little Girl snuggling with Rebecca.*

36

Pimples!

Your beauty should not come from outward adornment,
such as elaborate hairstyles and the wearing of
gold jewelry or fine clothes. Rather, it should be that of your
inner self, the unfading beauty of a gentle and quiet spirit,
which is of great worth in God's sight.

1 Peter 3:3-4

The door of my Dodge pickup groaned as I pushed it open and hopped out. My muck boots sloshed into the melting February snow. My heart fluttered. I couldn't wait to see my horses and mule. I'd moved to a different town more than 100 miles away, and until I settled into a permanent home, I was pasturing my critters at a friend's place. I hadn't seen them for several days. I heard the whinnies and brays of greeting as soon as I slammed the truck door.

I hurried over to the wooden corral, opened the green metal gate, and slipped through, shutting it behind me. My tall, black mare, Dazzle, was the first to greet me by nuzzling my jacket and asking to be petted. I ruffled her long winter coat. "Hi, silly girl. It's so good to see you too. I missed you!" I ran my hand down her neck to her favorite spot to be scratched and dug my fingernails in. She stretched her neck like a giraffe and leaned into the pressure, wanting me to push harder. As I did, I noticed that she had bumps all over her neck and chest...little pointy bumps. I leaned forward. With my hands I parted her long hair. Pimples? And she was covered with them.

I oozed with sympathy. "Oh, Dazzle, I'm so sorry." This had happened before when I'd switched her hay or when she'd gone through an unsettling transition, such as moving to a different pasture. The black mare continued to lean into my fingers. I sighed. "You're such a sensitive horse. You're so much like I was when I was a teenager."

Instantly my thoughts drifted back to those painful years. I don't know if it was the food I ate, the hormones coursing through my body, or my daily emotional swings, but my teen years were filled with zits. I tried everything to mask those little pointy bumps, pop them, or get rid of them. Nothing seemed to work. And the more pimples I had, and the longer I had them, the uglier I felt. During those dark days I'd ride my bike out to the pasture to visit my sorrel horse, Andy. He was my first horse, and he always raced to the fence to greet me. He didn't care if I had pimples. He loved me for who I was. Through his acceptance, I figured out that I couldn't change the zits on the outside, but I could be the best-looking person on the inside. That's what mattered most to God anyway.

A light, cold breeze brushed my cheek. "Dazzle, I wish I could make your pimples go away, but I can't. It's just going to take time for you to adjust to your new pasture." I wrapped my arms around her neck and gave her a big hug. "I love you!"

Dazzle curled her head down over my shoulder and pulled, drawing me closer to her, returning my hug.

Rebecca horsing around with Dazzle.
Notice Rebecca's muck boots.*

• Just Between You and Me •

Do you get zits? Have you had more than one or two at a time? It's embarrassing, isn't it? I thought that when I grew up I wouldn't get them anymore. Wrong! Sometimes I still do—and I'm a lot older than you.

I'm so grateful that I had my horse Andy during my teen years to comfort me and teach me the priceless lesson that I was loved regardless of what was happening to me physically. Through Andy, God demonstrated His priorities that are revealed in the Bible. You see, a person can dress up in cute clothes, wear the most fashionable makeup, and don dazzling jewelry, but that doesn't reflect who she really is inside. God doesn't care so much about the "fluff" of a person—what she looks like on the outside—because that doesn't always reflect the person's heart. What God wants is for us to draw close to Jesus and live to be more like Him—beautiful on the inside with kind and gentle hearts.

Lord, show us how to become more
beautiful in Your eyes. Amen.

• Just for Fun •

Did you know that an animal as big as a horse could be so sensitive that she would break out in pimples? Many animals are emotional just like you and I are. If their daily routine changes, they often get stressed out.

What are some things that keep horses relaxed and happy? One is having a scheduled feeding time, which means feeding them at the same times each day. I'm sure you feel better when you know your meals are going to happen around the same time every day too.

37

And...And...And?

*Worry is a heavy burden, but a
kind word always brings cheer.*

Proverbs 12:25 CEV

I nervously tapped my pen on the newspaper spread out in front of me. I rubbed my forehead. I'd just read every "help wanted" ad in the classifieds section, and I didn't find one that was close to what I needed. I took in shallow breaths as I reviewed my situation. I was worried. I was living in a new town, and for the last couple months I'd only found temporary jobs. To get by, I'd been housesitting for a friend so I wouldn't have to pay much rent. My mule and horses were in another friend's pasture nearby. I needed a permanent job that paid well so I could get my own place that included pasture and sheds for my animals and equipment. I couldn't live like this much longer.

I needed to get a fulltime job with a steady income. Only it wasn't that easy. All my animals made it complicated. Along with my mule and three horses (one pregnant), I owned a German shepherd and two cats. I'd need to rent a big place (and have really nice landlords who would let me have so many critters). Rent for a big place like that would probably be very expensive. None of the jobs I saw in the paper would pay enough. *And how am I going to find a place like that to live? They're almost impossible to find.*

I grabbed the keys to my truck and headed out the door. *I'll go down to the pasture and see the horses. I think better when I'm around them.* The tires on the truck splashed through the puddles on the highway. My knuckles were white from gripping the steering wheel so hard. My thoughts stampeded as I pleaded with my heavenly Father. *God, what if I can't find a job? How will I pay the pasture rent? And what about Dancer? It's already April, and she's going to give birth in July. And I've got to have money for veterinarian expenses.* The faster my thoughts raced, the worse I felt. Soon my stomach started hurting.

When I pulled into the driveway where I kept my mule and horses I was relieved. But that only lasted a few minutes. I hopped out of the truck and spotted Dancer. The sorrel mare stood in a field with new shoots of green grass. She was so round from her pregnancy now that she looked like someone had blown her up like a balloon. She recognized the truck and waddled over to the wooden fence.

I slipped through the gate and wrapped my arms around her neck in a hug. I confided, "Oh, Dancer, I want to have a place where all of you can live with me again. And I want to be with you when you have your baby." My heart sank even as the words came out. *How can I bring us all together when I can't even find a job or afford a place to live? And what am I going to do after the baby is born? I'll need a place safe enough for a baby.* The more I thought about the situation, the more impossible it became.

Suddenly I heard a cheery voice behind me.

"Hi, Rebecca!"

It was my friend Dena, who owned the pasture.

She beamed at me. "Dancer sure is getting big."

I nodded even as the tears leaked out the corners of my eyes. I poured out the worries that filled my heart.

When I finished, Dena merely said with a matter-of-fact voice, "Now, Rebecca, you know that everything always works out."

I gritted my teeth. She was right. I was disgusted with myself. *What had all that worrying done for me?* The thoughts had spun so fast through my mind that I hadn't even given God time to answer my prayers. Worrying had stopped me from seeking His answer.

During the next few minutes, Dena asked me questions and

helped me think of some possible jobs. After she left and I took care of my critters, I headed back to where I was housesitting. My heart felt lighter.

A couple days later Dena called. She said she'd found a job opportunity that I might be interested in. "Why don't you go apply?"

I did—and I got the job!

A few weeks later I excitedly trailered my "zoo" to my new job at a guest ranch. The owners said I could live on the ranch with all my animals, and they'd pay me to cook for the guests. It was the best solution to my impossible situation. Why had I doubted God? When I let the noise of worry drown out His voice, He continued to love me. In fact, He sent a friend to help me find His answer—a job as a cook on a ranch. How perfect!

• Just Between You and Me •

Do you wonder if you'll "fit in" with a new group of friends? And what if you don't pass the friendship test? And what if the kids in the school make fun of you or your clothes? And what if your new friends don't like horses? And...and...and. Have you ever noticed that the more you worry, the bigger the problems seem to become and the louder they scream—until they look like monsters that want to eat you up? Why do we let them grow that big? Why don't we stop them when they first pop into our minds? We can, you know. God tells us not to worry:

> Do not worry about your life, what you will eat or drink; or about your body, what you will wear. Is not life more than food, and the body more than clothes? Look at the birds of the air; they do not sow or reap or store away in barns, and yet your heavenly Father feeds them. Are you not much more valuable than they? (Matthew 6:25-26).

So how do we turn off worry? The key is to drop the thought as soon as it occurs. When a worry pops into your mind, consider it like a hot skillet that will burn you. Drop it immediately. Refuse to think about it. And if you have difficulty, ask God to help you. Trust Him to send the worry away. And, yes, sometimes you might have to do this more than once, but God will always help you. I'm going to work on doing that from now on. How about you?

Lord, when worry screams for our attention,
please remind us to drop that thought right away.
And if it refuses to leave, remind us to turn to You for help.
I know You'll comfort us...and You might even
send friends with wise and
cheerful words to encourage us. Thank You! Amen.

• Just for Fun •

Do you know how much horses weigh? It varies a lot depending on the breed. Do you know how much weight a mare gains during a normal pregnancy? Studies have shown that she gains 9 to 14 percent of her body weight. That means a horse that weighs 1200 pounds would gain 108 to 140 pounds. Isn't that amazing?

38

Doorknobs

*When I heard your greeting, the baby
in my womb jumped for joy.*

Luke 1:44 NLT

The brilliant pinks of the sunset flickered across the sky and over the mountains. The heat from the day had made the air dry, almost crispy. Two halters hung over my shoulder, the buckles jangling with each step I took. Small shuffling feet, stirring poofs of dust, followed me down the dirt road to the pasture. I felt like the "Pied Piper" of storybook fame as the children skipped along behind me.

I was working at the guest ranch, and this evening after dinner I'd gathered the guests' kids for a field trip. We trooped to the meadow where Dancer and Czar lived. After a long day cooking for 35 to 50 people, it was delightful to watch the children enjoy my pregnant mare. Never in a million years would I have guessed what was going to happen.

Czar and Dancer plucked long stems of grass and chewed as they watched us top the hill above the pasture. I raised my voice over the chatter. "Now, kids, do you remember what we need to do?"

All eyes turned toward me.

I held my finger to my mouth to signal a hush. "Nobody can say a word until I tell you. Not one. Okay?" All the little heads bobbed. This had been the game I'd played nearly every night since I'd moved to the ranch.

39

The Blimp

You grew tall and matured as a woman.

Ezekiel 16:7 MSG

The sun glinted off the surface of the lake in Czar and Dancer's pasture. The two horses lay sprawled close to the shore, taking their afternoon naps. As soon as they heard me wading through the waist-deep grass, they groggily lifted their heads and squinted in the bright sunlight. Even though Dancer wasn't due to foal for a couple weeks, every break I had from my job at the guest ranch I slipped down to the pasture wondering, *Is today the day?* I scanned the sea of grass that waved in the summer breeze, but I didn't see any little ears.

I cupped my hands to my mouth and shouted, "C'mon!"

Czar stood up. His bay coat glistened as he shook. Fine particles of dust floated in a cloud around him. Dancer rolled onto her belly and grunted as she gathered her hind legs underneath her and moved her front legs in front of her. Heaving, she stood and braced herself with all four legs angled to prop her up. She was so round from her pregnancy that she looked like she might pop. I giggled. *You're as big the Goodyear Blimp! Wind Dancer definitely hasn't come yet. She's still ide you.*

Dancer walked toward me, her belly swinging side-to-side like a dulum. With his nose, Czar nudged her from behind, telling her rry up.

shook my head at him. "Czar, I don't think she can move any Can't you see her waddle?" Walking to meet them, I eyed the

The tall grass swished as we tiptoed to the pasture. Czar sauntered over to the gate. Dancer waddled behind him. I lifted the gate handle and shoed the children through. I followed and latched the gate. After slipping halters on the horses, I pointed to my eyes and mouthed, "Watch me."

I leaned my face against Dancer's flank. I motioned for the children to line up on both sides of Dancer and do the same thing. Whispering, I said, "Okay, kids, the baby's going to kick when I talk to her. You'll be able to feel the baby move, so get ready." I pressed my face into Dancer's warm and furry flank. All was still inside the womb. Nothing stirred. In a singsong voice I said loudly, "Hi, Wind Dancer. How was your day?"

Wind Dancer kicked...and kicked. It was like she was playing the drums.

The children squealed.

I coached them. "You can talk to the baby now."

They pushed their round faces into Dancer's sides. All at the same time, they chattered.

Suddenly the kids screamed. Horrifying, blood curdling wails!

I stepped back and blinked in amazement. *Wow!* From inside the womb, the baby who was lying on her back with her feet pointed in the air, had pushed. She'd pushed so hard with her front feet that a lump appeared on either side of her mom's flank. The lumps stuck out like doorknobs! The outline of her hooves showed. The children howled like it was a monster and turned to run away. I shouted, "Kids, stop! Don't be scared. It's just the baby."

The air was still for a couple seconds while the kids stopped, turned, and stared at the lumps...then at me...then back at the lumps. Finally, one of the children squealed with delight, "It's a baby!"

My heart raced. Carefully, I squeezed one of the tiny hooves. The baby let me hold it. I shouted, "C'mon, kids! I think she wants you to touch her."

One by one the kids held Wind Dancer's hooves. When they'd all taken their turn squeezing, it was as if Wind Dancer knew. She quit pushing, and the lumps disappeared.

While we walked up the dirt road to the lodge, the children couldn't quit giggling and talking about the baby. Not me. I was caught up in my own world. I'd just witnessed a baby in the womb wanting to communicate with people on the outside. It was a miracle I'll never forget.

• Just Between You and Me •

Did you know that your mother could feel you move inside of her before you were born? Babies in the womb are very active. When they're small they even swim because the sac they're in is filled with fluid. An ultrasound can detect a baby's movement when it's just seven or eight weeks old. But moms usually don't feel their babies move until they're bigger, usually between 16 to 22 weeks old.

Some moms say that the movement of the baby feels like butterflies in their tummies or even like there is popcorn popping in there. Did you know that sometimes when human babies are in the womb they push their feet out like Wind Dancer did? Their moms can see the outline of the little feet!

In today's Bible verse, the baby in the womb who jumped for joy became a very famous man in biblical times. Even while still in the womb, he created such a stir that his mother commented about it. Who was he? John the Baptist, who prepared the way for Jesus. You can read more about John in Luke 1:39-45.

Lord, thank You for showing us how much
of a miracle a baby is. Amen.

• Just for Fun •

Have you ever heard of "imprinting a foal"? It's a process of introducing a newborn horse or mule to the world around it. Many trainers strongly believe that by imprinting the foal, it will be easier to train and it will trust people more. What I did with Wind Dancer was similar, only it was while she was still in the womb.

For fun, why don't you type "imprint a foal" on the Internet to find out more?

mare. Her body had undergone lots of clunky and awkward changes. Her belly was kind of v-shaped and hung so low it looked like she could use a skateboard underneath it to hold her up. She walked as if she was wearing diapers. As she got closer I noticed that her udder had grown larger.

Dancer stopped in front of me. She closed her eyes as I rubbed the white blaze on her forehead. "Dancer, only God knows the exact time when you're going to give birth, but we're one day closer."

Dancer.

• Just Between You and Me •

When human women grow round with their babies, their bodies undergo clunky and awkward changes too. Many are similar to what I noticed with Dancer. Just like with Dancer, no one except God knows the timing of a baby's birth (unless there are complications that require surgery). Doctors give people a general time based on averages, and many women guess, but only God knows the exact moment.

Being pregnant isn't the only time our bodies go through awkward changes. I remember the horrible time I had when I was first becoming a woman. It was obvious in the locker room during gym class that some of the girls' bodies were already changing into adult form, but mine hadn't. Often they would tease me, and I'd be embarrassed.

At the time I didn't realize that God was the One who determined when that would happen. I just knew there wasn't anything I could do about it. Knowing more about God now, I wish I could go back and relive those years. Instead of being embarrassed, I'd be content and enjoy the miracle of God gradually transforming me into a woman. I hope you take the time to appreciate the amazing changes God is bringing about in you and that you're trusting His timing.

Lord, help us enjoy even the awkward days of growing into the women You want us to be. Amen.

• Just for Fun •

A few days after this, Dakota, one of the cowgirls at the ranch, sat down at the dinner table. After hanging her cowboy hat on her knee, she leaned back in her chair and looked at me.

"Hey, Reba (that's my nickname), that mare of yours is going to foal in the next 48 hours."

I shrugged off her comment by saying, "She's not due for a couple weeks."

Dakota confidently leaned forward. "You watch. She will."

Why was Dakota so sure she knew when Dancer would foal (give birth)? Type "predicting foaling" into the Internet to see if you can figure it out. I also put three big clues in this chapter. Write down what you think they are. (You can confirm your answers by looking at page 157.)

40

The Answer

[Jesus'] sheep follow him because they know his voice.

John 10:4

The sounds of clattering dishes filled the lodge as the crew cleared the breakfast table. The current guests' vacation stays had come to an end. Today was the day they'd all leave. I sat at the table saying goodbye to my new friends and exchanging phone numbers and addresses so we could keep in touch. Even though Dancer's due date was a couple weeks away, all of them had hoped Dancer would give birth while they were here. Now they wanted me to promise to send photos of Wind Dancer as soon as it happened.

Every evening during their stay, many of the guests' children had trooped down the dirt road to the pasture with me so they could press their rosy cheeks into Dancer's belly and talk to the baby. They'd skip back to their parents with stories of how the baby would be quiet until she heard their voices, and then she'd kick up a storm. Wind Dancer had become famous—and she wasn't even born yet!

The question on most minds, including mine, was whether Wind Dancer would recognize my voice after she was born. They'd been hoping to see for themselves. *When she's out of the womb, will Wind Dancer know my voice?* I wondered almost all the time.

Suddenly the heavy wooden front door swung open and thumped the wall. We all turned and stared at Ashely. She was one of the guests who had supposedly headed home. She excitedly shouted across the room. "Reba, did you know Dancer had her baby?"

I looked at her in shock. "My baby's on the ground?"

Ashely scooped her arm toward the pasture. "C'mon!"

Everyone in the dining room screamed. I grabbed my camera, and we all thundered down the dirt road to the pasture. *Will she know me?* raced through my mind. For the last ten-and-a-half months I'd been talking to Wind Dancer in the womb and singing her a little song nearly every day. The past couple months at the guest ranch Wind Dancer had heard lots of different voices, and she'd always responded.

I ran down the dirt road. It was a long way from the lodge to the pasture. The guests straggled behind. My breath came in gasps and my legs ached. I pushed on. *Will she know me?* In the back of my mind I heard the voices of mule breeders who had cautioned me about my expectations. I'd been talking with them about training Wind Dancer. When I mentioned the games I'd been playing with her, they shook their heads and scowled. "You have to remember she's a *mule*. Mules are very different than horses. Mules are wild when they're born. If they're in a field, once they get their feet underneath them, you'll never catch them...at least not for the first couple weeks."

I topped the hill and scanned the pasture while running to the fence. A sorrel-colored foal stood on wobbly legs next to Dancer! Czar stood by Dancer's side, glancing to and fro. He was obviously guarding the baby. I stopped at the rail fence and handed my camera to Ashely, who was right behind me.

"Will you please take some pictures?" I asked hurriedly.

The other guests arrived and whispered as they spread out and sat on the wooden rails. They settled in to see what was going to happen.

My heart thumped wildly like a drumroll. I slid between the wooden rails. If I was too full of energy, Dancer might pick up on it and get too nervous to let me near her foal. Momentarily I paused, closed my eyes, and took a deep breath. I opened my eyes and calmly strode toward Dancer. The baby was wobbling to the other side of her mom so I couldn't see her. Dancer looked exhausted. Her head drooped, and she could barely keep her eyes open.

Slowly I stepped toward her. Standing at her shoulder, I said, "Hi, Dancer." For a few moments, I gently stroked her forehead. "What a beautiful baby you have, girl."

Suddenly I felt a nudge at my side. I looked down just as Wind Dancer slipped between my arm and my body and stood there. *She knows me! She's not doing the wild-mule thing at all. She's recognizing my voice!* I wanted to shout to everyone, "Wind Dancer knows my voice!" Even through she'd never seen me, when she heard my voice she walked around her mom to find me. *The experiment worked!*

Rebecca and Wind Dancer's first "in person" meeting
with Dancer supervising.

• Just Between You and Me •

Did you think Wind Dancer would know my voice after she was born? Even though I'd never heard of anyone doing in-the-womb imprinting for a foal, I'd talked with Wind Dancer when she was still in Dancer's womb all those months. I believed it would make a difference. Why did I believe this so strongly? Because Wind Dancer's life started the moment she was conceived, and I'd been present then and every step of the way. Even though she couldn't see me and I couldn't see her, we'd become friends. She heard me singing and talking, and when she'd grown some, she'd kick in answer. Why would that change after she was born? Well, once she was born I didn't want her kicking every time she heard my voice. But I was ecstatic to have her snuggle next to my body.

The success of the imprinting experiment got me thinking about the verses in the Bible that talk about God forming us in our mother's womb. (Why not look up and read Psalm 139:13-16 and Isaiah 44:2?) God was present the very moments you and I were conceived. He was there the whole time, fashioning us into who we would become. God watched us while we were in the womb. So wouldn't it be natural for us to know His voice?

Lord, we want to hear Your voice clearly.
Show us how. Amen.

• Just for Fun •

When a foal is born, how long do you think it takes for it to stand up and walk? A foal is usually able to stand on its wobbly legs and get milk from its mom 30 minutes to 3 hours after its born.

Are you wondering why that's such a long time frame? Have you ever seen a foal try to stand up for the first time? It's funny and amazing at the same time. Remember, a foal's never been able to stretch its legs before. Go to YouTube and check out "newborn foals walking."

41

Is She Okay?

*I pray that the Lord will guide you to be as
loving as God and as patient as Christ.*

2 Thessalonians 3:5 CEV

Wind Dancer leaned her warm, reddish-brown body against my leg. I stroked her neck. Only moments before I'd met her for the first time outside of the womb, and she'd recognized my voice. I looked down and took inventory to make sure she was okay. The tips of her long ears curled inward. Her short, curly, red mane fluttered in the light breeze. She was so skinny I could see the outline of each one of her ribs, which was normal for a newborn foal. My eyes wandered down her spindly legs, and then I gasped. She wasn't standing correctly. On her front legs, at her fetlock joints (her front ankles), her hooves were bent at a strange angle so her hooves stuck out in front of her, a bit like clown shoes would. My mouth went dry. *Oh no! What's wrong? Will she be okay?*

Suddenly Wind Dancer shook her head and darted from under my arm. She shifted her hind legs and dashed around her mom in wobbly circles. I cringed with each stride, watching her bound with her fetlocks touching the ground. *Ouch! That must hurt,* I thought. As suddenly as she started, she skidded to a stop next to her mom's flank. She reached under her mom, butted her mom's udder, latched on, and slurped down fresh milk.

Sweat beaded on my forehead. *God, is she deformed?* I called the veterinary clinic. Over the next couple hours while I waited for the veterinarian to come to the pasture, my thoughts bucked and kicked through horrible possibilities. I wanted to find out what the doctor had to say, but then I didn't. What if he said she was deformed and would never be okay? What would I do?

Finally the clinic's white truck pulled down the dirt driveway and parked by the pasture. I swallowed hard as I watched the doctor slip through the wooden rails and walk down the hill toward me. We shook hands and then he eyed Wind Dancer, who was standing by her mom's side.

"That's a nice-looking foal," he said.

I nodded.

We chatted for a few minutes about Dancer, and he coached me on what I could do to help her recover from the stresses of giving birth.

I couldn't wait any longer. My tummy was getting upset, so I finally asked, "What's wrong with the foal's legs? Will she be okay?"

He scrunched his eyebrows and watched the colt. "What was the due date?"

I paused as my mind computed the numbers. "She was born two weeks early."

The vet rubbed his stubbly beard. "Mules are often born two weeks later than horse foals. That means altogether she might be three to four weeks early." He suddenly grinned as he explained that because she was a bit premature in being born, she hadn't fully developed *yet*. "Be patient, Rebecca. Her legs will strengthen, and she'll walk just fine."

A wave of relief washed over me. All I had to do was be patient! Wind Dancer was going to be okay.

Wind Dancer was healthy except her fetlock and
pastern joints weren't fully developed.

• Just Between You and Me •

Have you been told to be patient? How did you respond?

Did you know that "being patient" means more than just waiting for time to pass? It also means to be still with your thoughts, especially when you're facing trouble. In other words, don't let your imagination go wild and build drama *before* any drama happens. Instead, keep your thoughts calm and peaceful.

Over the next few days I watched Wind Dancer stumble around the pasture. She was full of energy. There were times that thoughts of her being permanently crippled slipped into my mind. How could I keep my thoughts steady when fear kept trying to come into my heart?

Wind Dancer's temporary handicap didn't slow her down at all.

I knew God gives His followers the ability and strength to choose what we think if we ask Him, so I did. Then I chose to focus solely on the answer He gave me through the vet. Wind Dancer would be fine. Anytime fear reared its ugly head, I sent it away. I refused to let the words "deformed" and "crippled" enter my thoughts and take up brain space.

In just a few weeks, Wind Dancer was prancing around the pasture on perfect legs and hooves.

Lord, show us how to be patient and
depend on You. Amen.

• Just for Fun •

How premature can a baby horse be born and still have a good chance to survive and be healthy? A "normal" due date after a foal is conceived is around 11 months. The foal will usually have a good chance of survival and health if it's 9½ to 10 months along (1½ months early).

How premature can a human baby be born and survive and be healthy? Human babies have a normal due date of 9 months. Some people say babies can be born 3 months early and survive with the proper care.

Two important things to remember when it comes to premature births: 1) There are exceptions to every general rule, and 2) our God performs miracles. He's in the miracle business.

42

The Lake

*You are my friend, and you are
my fortress where I am safe.*

Psalm 144:2 CEV

The tall grass in the pasture gently swayed in the light breeze. Sweat rolled down my back. Czar, my ancient bay horse, stood next to his girlfriend, Dancer. The mare, having given birth to Wind Dancer several hours before, stood exhausted, her head drooping and her eyelids sagging shut. Wind Dancer slurped milk and shifted her weight back and forth, acting like it was a bother to stop to drink. She'd rather be romping around her new world exploring.

With my hand I shielded my eyes from the afternoon sun. *Do I dare leave for a few hours and fence off a new pasture for her?* Although Wind Dancer's legs weren't totally developed yet, she stampeded around the pasture. When she turned downhill, it looked like her speed topped a Kentucky Derby racehorse. Her wobbly legs seemed to fly in all directions, but they carried her forward.

I shook my head in frustration. Having been born up to four weeks early for a mule, she'd caught me by surprise. I'd planned on fencing off a smaller, safer pasture for her nursery, but I hadn't had a chance to do that. Instead, my baby mule had been born in a huge pasture that had a lake. And the lake was at the bottom of the hill she was racing up and down. *If she tears down the hill, she might not be able to stop in time. If she flies into the lake, she could get stuck in the muddy bottom and drown. God, do I dare leave her so I can fence the new pasture?*

I sighed as I watched my critters. The sun glinted off Czar's shiny coat as he cropped grass and slowly moved down the hill. Dancer looked as if she was so tired she might fall over. Wind Dancer butted her mom's udder, took a couple more slurps, and then pulled her head out from under her mom. She glanced around, switched her little fuzzy tail, and burst into a gallop. She orbited around her mom. The circle kept getting bigger and bigger. As she became more confident, she galloped further and further down the hill.

Wind Dancer eyeing the lake when Dancer's not looking.

I tilted my head and watched Czar wander down the hill. *What's he doing?* He now stood about 50 feet from the shoreline, facing uphill. Then I noticed something I'd never seen before. He'd positioned himself to block the little mule filly from the lake—to protect her from danger. Every time Wind Dancer flew down the slope, Czar glared at her. As she got closer, he pinned his ears and bobbed his head, which is daddy horse language for "Don't go any further young'un or you'll get a spanking." Instantly she'd turn and run uphill toward her mom.

Czar keeping Wind Dancer away from the lake.

I chuckled as I watched Wind Dancer cruise a couple more rounds toward the lake. She gave up on the idea and explored the uphill pasture. Czar dropped his head and cropped grass along the shoreline. God had worked it out. Czar would stand guard so I could get to work on fencing a smaller pasture.

• Just Between You and Me •

Have you considered that God not only watches over us, but He also watches over the animals we care about? Czar being Wind Dancer's guardian is a great example. Why does God do that? Because He loves His creation. Why does He protect you and me? Because he loves us so much that He wants to protect us from harm. He wants to be our true friend.

How has God been *your* friend?

Lord, help us to see the many ways You protect us because You love us. Amen.

• Just for Fun •

Did you know that horses are natural swimmers? They don't have to be taught how to swim, but they do need to be given opportunities to swim before they'll become sure of themselves in the water. Like us, they need experience to know how to stay safe and avoid muddy shores and lake bottoms.

Did you know that there are swimming pools made especially for horses? On the Internet, type in "horse pool" and see all the interesting things listed.

43

Strong Arms

[God said,] "I have made you and I will carry you;
I will sustain you and I will rescue you."

Isaiah 46:4

The dining room in the lodge was alive with sounds of the guests chattering as they finished eating. I sat at the table with the crew, wrestling with my thoughts. Wind Dancer had been born in a pasture with a lake. I was concerned she might accidentally run into the lake, get stuck in the mud, and drown, so I'd fenced off a smaller pasture up on the hill next to my horse trailer where I knew she'd be safe.

All day I'd been fighting the coming problem. *How am I going to move her?* Caught up in my own world, I propped my elbows on the table and rested my chin in my hands. At wit's end, I sighed. *God, what am I going to do?*

Everyone at my table grew quiet.

Amber, a wrangler sitting next to me, asked, "Is everything okay?"

I nodded and faked a smile. Without taking a breath I fired off my problem. "I just finished fencing a nursery for Wind Dancer. Now I'm trying to figure out how to move her up there. She doesn't have a clue how to lead. I could put a halter on her mom and let Wind Dancer romp freely, but I'm not sure she'd follow that well. She's so interested in the world around her that she could take off at the speed of a bullet. Who knows what kind of trouble she might get into?" I nervously twirled my long braid and continued. "And it's not like the nursery is close by. I bet it's a quarter mile away. I can't carry her that far. Besides, she wouldn't like being picked up. I'm not strong enough to hold her if she fights." My body sagged as I sighed again.

Chance, who was built like a weight lifter, leaned forward. The muscles in his arms rippled as he rested them on the table. "I can carry her."

I looked up and I'm sure my eyes sparkled. "Really?"

After cleaning up dishes, we walked down to the pasture. Two halters hung from my shoulder. Czar and Dancer nickered when they saw us coming. The foal raced in circles around them. Little clods of dirt flew from her tiny hooves. I buckled the halters on the adult horses and held their lead ropes while we waited for Wind Dancer to settle down and nurse. When she did, Chance stepped next to her. As soon as she licked the last drops of milk from her lips, he scooped her into his arms and heaved her off the ground.

The little foal's eyes grew wide. The whites around them showed. Wind Dancer struggled to get free. She swung her head side-to-side and flailed her legs like a windmill. Chance's face grew red and the veins stood out on his forehead as he struggled to hold the baby. The muscles in his strong arms bulged. The foal bucked and kicked. As a last resort because she couldn't get free, she screamed a frantic, high-pitched mule honk to her mom.

I tightened my hold on Dancer's lead rope, worried that motherly instinct might kick in and she'd get mad at Chance. But she merely stood and watched, confident that we weren't going to hurt her baby.

As suddenly as Wind Dancer started her fight, she gave up and sagged in Chance's arms. She rested her head over his shoulder and looked at me as if to say, "Okay, let's get on with it."

Chance hiked up the hill. I chuckled as I led Czar and Dancer. Wind Dancer's behavior reminded me of myself. I raced around life full-speed ahead, running from adventure to adventure to explore the world, trying to do things on my own. When I came up against hard things, my mind would kick and buck until I finally gave up and asked God for help—not unlike today, I admitted. I'd tried to figure out how to move Wind Dancer all by myself. When I came to the end of myself, I asked God. But that's not what God really wants. He didn't want me working independently from Him, turning to Him only when I got stuck. No, He wants me to walk safely by His side *all the time*. And when things get hard, He wants to carry me to safety just like Chance carried Wind Dancer.

When Chance set Wind Dancer down in her new pasture, instead of running away she cuddled up next to him. Over the next couple weeks, every time Wind Dancer spied Chance she'd bray a high-pitched "heeeee haaawww" until Chance walked over to the nursery and scratched her. Wind Dancer's trust in Chance had grown when she'd relaxed in the safety of his strong arms and nothing bad had happened. I needed to do the same thing—work on building my trust in God while He holds me in His powerful love.

Wind Dancer having breakfast.

• Just Between You and Me •

When you face a hard decision or a tough project, do you usually try to figure things out by yourself? I've done this so many times. Afterward I think, *Since God knows the perfect answer to everything, and He wants me to win in life, why didn't I stop and ask Him before I barged ahead full speed?*

When I was contemplating moving Wind Dancer, if I'd stopped worrying and fighting for an answer, and, instead, chosen to relax in God's strong arms, I'm sure He would have told me to ask Chance for help. How simple that would have been, and so much better than being upset all morning trying to figure out how to move the colt.

Maybe this is something you and I can both work on. Next time, as soon as things get hard and we get upset, let's stop and ask God to scoop us into His loving arms and let us know what to do.

Lord, when we face difficult stuff, please remind us to let You carry us. Amen.

• Just for Fun •

After a foal is born, how long should you wait before you start training it? You can start right away with very simple things like imprinting and getting the colt used to a halter. I buckled a halter on Wind Dancer shortly after she was born. You can find out more about training foals by going to the Internet and typing "training newborn foals."

44

King of the Hill

Yes, we should make the most of what God gives,
both the bounty and the capacity to enjoy it,
accepting what's given and delighting in the work.

Ecclesiastes 5:19 MSG

A few ravens cawed as they flew overhead. The hot sun beat down on me, and sweat beaded on my forehead. I sat on a plastic stepstool outside my long, white horse trailer, watching Wind Dancer nurse. She stomped her foot and impatiently butted her mom's udder. She was sucking so hard I could hear her slurping. I'd just fenced off this small pasture around the horse trailer, and a few minutes ago Chance had carried Wind Dancer into this new pasture.

Sweat dribbled down the center of my back. I glanced around the area I'd nicknamed "the nursery." Although it was a safe spot for Wind Dancer, it was small and flat except for the four-foot-high and 10-foot-round pile of dirt that was leftover from one of the ranch's construction projects. *God, this place looks boring. What is Wind Dancer going to do all day? She needs to explore and play, but there's not much here. There's not even a tree in here to run circles around. She doesn't have any playmates either. I wish I had something better for her.*

Wind Dancer pulled her head from under her mom. Milk dribbled off her long, curly whiskers. Her short and wispy red mane stood on end. She cocked her head side-to-side as she surveyed her new home. She stretched out her neck and snuffled the tall grass. Cautiously she strutted along the fence line exploring, until she'd completed the perimeter. Her mom followed closely behind.

Then the foal spotted the mound of dirt in the center. She lowered her head, pinned her ears back, and slowly stalked over to it. She sniffed the dirt and pawed it. Suddenly she switched her fuzzy tail, gathered on her haunches, and galloped up the hill. She stopped at the top, arched her neck, and proudly thrust out her chest as if to say, "Look at me!"

Wind Dancer awkwardly stepped off the top, not sure how to use her wobbly legs for going down a dirt hill. She pedaled and skidded to the bottom before flattening into an all-out run around her new pasture. She bucked and kicked and snorted as she passed me. On her second lap, she turned toward the center and scampered up the dirt pile. Once again she proudly paused at the top before slip-sliding to the bottom.

Wind Dancer having a great time.

Delighted, I laughed. She was using the boring pasture as an opportunity to play the game "King of the Hill." She'd taken the little she had and turned it into fun. I brushed a few stray strands of my blond hair behind my ear. *God, I guess it doesn't matter what's in the pasture. Either it can be boring or it can be fun. It's all about the way a mule looks at it.*

Over the next few weeks Wind Dancer's legs got stronger. She looked like a reigning horse in competition as she played King of the Hill. She'd spin on her haunches and dodge and weave as she leaped up and down the mound. Who knew that a plain old mound of dirt could be so much fun? Hour after hour I watched her romp. I thought of how God had taken my mistake of buying Dancer without asking Him first and shown me how to take the shattered pieces and make them into a beautiful dream. He'd given me the gift of this foal—a gift of life—to enjoy and to have fun with. Who knew that a broken horse could bring such a blessing?

I knew Wind Dancer and I would have lots of years to share our dreams. I wouldn't trade her for the world.

• Just Between You and Me •

Have you ever been totally bored? Bored with class, bored with friends, bored with family, bored at home? Perhaps life isn't really boring—it's the way you're looking at it that makes it seem dreary. Wind Dancer taught me that there are opportunities to have fun anywhere and everywhere. Life is a gift God gives us, and it's up to us to take advantage of opportunities to relish it.

How could you have more fun without changing anything except the way you think? Why not try it now?

Lord, show us how to create an exciting life
filled with You in everything we do. Amen.

• Just for Fun •

Do you know why foals play? God gave them that nature so they can develop their muscles, improve their coordination, and get their minds going. Have you watched foals romp around? I could watch them for hours! You can too by going to YouTube.com and typing in "foals playing."

All Grown Up

I'm excited about the years that Wind Dancer and I have ahead of us. She's grown up now, and she loves to entertain. I think it's because of all the attention she received during the pregnancy. Once she was born, she became the star of the guest ranch. The guests' children mugged her, and Wind Dancer ate it up.

God certainly made my dreams come true—and He'll do the same for you. I know it.

A grown-up Wind Dancer giving Rebecca a kiss.*

Wind Dancer learned to say "thank you"
from her mom, Dancer.*

Want to Join God's Family?

Jesus replied, "I tell you the truth, unless you are born again, you cannot see the Kingdom of God."

John 3:3 NLT

Well, my friend, I hope you enjoyed reading these true stories about my horse and mule family. Are you as horse crazy as I am? Through my horses and mules I've learned a lot about Jesus and how much He loves having me be part of His family. Did you know that He wants you to be part of His family too? Have you asked Him to come into your heart and be your Savior? If not, would you like to invite Him into your life right now? It's not hard. In fact, it's pretty simple. You just need to ask Him! One way is to read this prayer out loud and believe it with all your heart. Jesus is listening for your voice!

> Jesus, thank You for dying on the cross to pay for my sins. I've done some things that are wrong. I'm sorry. Please forgive me for all of them and wash my heart clean. I believe You died on the cross for my sins, and You rose from the dead and are now living in heaven. I want You to be my Savior. Please come into my heart and change it—and me. Help me to trust You and follow You forever. Amen.

Congratulations on becoming part of God's family! And guess what...by believing in Jesus, you and I are now "sisters in Christ." Awesome!

• Just Between You and Me •

If you said this prayer or talked to God with all your heart for the first time, I'm so excited for you. I'm glad I can welcome you into God's family. What do you do next? Tell someone you know who believes in Jesus too. And then go to a church that teaches from the Bible and be baptized. I hope you and your friends will encourage each other to grow in Jesus.

Above all, remember that God loves you with all His heart...and so do I. You can visit me through my website: www.rebeccaondov .com. See you there!

Rebecca

P.S. If you didn't fill out the "Bill of Sale" to Christ, right now is a great time to do it. You can find it on page 22.

Answers for Chapter 39

Signs Indicating a Foal Will Be Born Soon

Here are three clues that helped Dakota guess when Dancer was going to foal (have her baby).

Clue 1: Dancer's belly was kind of v-shaped. This is caused by the baby repositioning itself to be born. Horse babies must turn over so they're right-side up with their heads facing toward the mom's rear. This stretches the mother's belly so it hangs lower than normal.

Clue 2: Dancer walked like she was wearing a diaper. Mares waddle, and just before they give birth their gait is even more awkward because the baby is moving even closer to the mom's rear end—getting into position to be delivered.

Clue 3: Dancer's udder was bigger. A mare's udder holds milk. Dancer's body was producing milk so her foal could get nourishment soon after it was born.